CW00797861

7/14 f5

CHELTENHAM'S
Lost Heritage

OLIVER C. BRADBURY
FOREWORD BY SIR HOWARD COLVIN FBA

SUTTON PUBLISHING

Sutton Publishing Limited
Phoenix Mill · Thrupp · Stroud
Gloucestershire · GL5 2BU

First published 2004

Copyright © Oliver C. Bradbury, 2004

Title page photograph: A detail of 33 Swindon
Road, *c.* 1939.

British Library Cataloguing in Publication Data
A catalogue record for this book is available from the
British Library.

ISBN 0-7509-2990-1

Typeset in 10.5/13.5 Photina.
Typesetting and origination by
Sutton Publishing Limited.
Printed and bound in England by
J.H. Haynes & Co. Ltd, Sparkford.

In memory of Alice Eugene Robbins
and Nigel Temple

The Elizabethan classroom scene pictured here is from a 1586 indenture for Pate's Grammar School.
It is thought to be the earliest pictorial representation of Cheltenham.

CONTENTS

FOREWORD

In the course of the last 250 years Cheltenham has undergone three transformations: in the eighteenth century from a small market town to a sophisticated watering place; in the mid-nineteenth from a declining spa to a fashionable residential town; and in the twentieth from a population largely of retired well-to-do people to one devoted to commerce, insurance, education, government communications and other businesses.

These changes have not been accomplished without architectural casualties. Of the market town virtually nothing remains except the medieval parish church; of the spa only one pump-room remains in use. In the twentieth century the transformation of villas into offices, of gardens into car parks, of individual shops into chainstores progressively eroded the character of the nineteenth-century residential town. Here an ungainly tower block destroyed the scale of an early nineteenth-century street, there the mechanical grid of a large office block rudely confronted the Gothic front of a Victorian college. Only very recently has a new development such as the carefully detailed Montpellier Apartments made a serious attempt to carry on the urban traditions of the past.

It is to Cheltenham's architectural losses that Oliver Bradbury's book is devoted. In the Age of Conservation his systematic record of architecture destroyed or mutilated in the past makes sad reading. Not all the lost buildings were architecturally important: what is more shocking than the losses is the abysmal quality of so many of those that replaced them. By systematically juxtaposing images of the old and the new Oliver Bradbury has shown the consistently poor quality of ordinary twentieth-century urban architecture in a place like Cheltenham where every effort should have been made to create something that would enhance rather than degrade it. This, then, is both a valuable historical record of what has been lost in the past, and a warning to the architects and planners of the twenty-first century to avoid the failures of the past hundred years.

Sir Howard Colvin FBA
Emeritus Fellow of St John's College, Oxford

INTRODUCTION

At a conservative estimate, some 350 to 400 buildings of historic consequence have been lost to Cheltenham over the last two centuries. Although this is only a fraction of the town's building stock, it has certainly left a visual impression of complete devastation in parts – municipal car parks immediately spring to mind. *Cheltenham's Lost Heritage* is a selective and in the process subjective, but I hope representative, account of the town's architectural losses. It has been written both for the people of Cheltenham and at a national level for architectural historians and conservationists. This publication, a gazetteer of sorts, intends to be a sobering and at the same time aesthetically rewarding account of the town's losses. There is no hidden reactionary agenda here: the book does not advocate the propagation of neo-Regency architecture as the solution to our current architectural impasse.

In some ways *Cheltenham's Lost Heritage* expands on Timothy Mowl's *Cheltenham Betrayed* (1995), but whereas the latter reproduced only ten destroyed buildings, this publication showcases well over 100 properties. *Cheltenham Betrayed* was often about the parties responsible for demolition, but *Cheltenham's Lost Heritage* is the pictorial requiem – perhaps an urban equivalent to *The Destruction of the Country House* (1974). In years to come it might hopefully fit into Robert Bargery, Secretary of the Georgian Group's categorisation: 'of those landmark laments for lost buildings – Fergusson on Bath, Lloyd *et al* on the City of London, Mowl on Cheltenham and Amery & Cruickshank on the whole of Britain'. The aim of *Cheltenham's Lost Heritage* is not to criticise the agents of demolition. This has been done before, and so one could argue that to criticise – at least emotively – is a cliché in itself.

CHELTENHAM'S HISTORICAL BACKGROUND

Cheltenham, a town by the thirteenth century, effectively reinvented itself in the eighteenth century, with the discovery of a source of medicinal spring waters in 1716. None the less development was painfully slow, and by 1781 only one house could be singled out in the guidebook of that year – this being 'The Cottage'; a property which was to evolve some forty years later into one of the town's most distinguished buildings – The Priory. In 1781 Cheltenham consisted 'principally of one regular, spacious and handsome street, about a mile in length' – this being the High Street. Cheltenham's meteoric success began with the visit of George III in 1788, during which the King stayed at Lord Fauconberg's house, Bayshill Lodge. By 1821 the *Cheltenham Chronicle* could, perhaps a little complacently, inform its readers of the 'elegance of our buildings [and] the tasteful diversity of our public Walks'. Of the town's recent rapid success, the *Chronicle* calculated that: 'We have seen that, about twenty years since, the number of houses did not exceed 710, whilst the inhabitants amounted but to 2,000: – By the late Census taken in June of the present year, there were 2,416 houses, and 13,388 inhabitants. How vast an increase!'

Although Cheltenham expanded greatly from the 1820s onwards, a series of not unimportant villas, widely scattered all over town, had been built during the first decade of the nineteenth century; most, unfortunately, have gone. An 1803 guidebook reflected, somewhat instructively, that: 'Great improvements have been made within the last ten years; many elegant rows and single houses have been erected, and others are now building.' Edward Mitchell's elegant 'Town of Cheltenham' map of 1806 enables us to identify these widely scattered villas: St Margaret's; Cox's Cottage (later The Priory); Cambray Pavilion and House; Lindsay Cottage; Grove Cottage; and so on: the point being that there were not many at this stage. In 1812 it was noted that 'within the last thirty years [the town] has been almost totally renewed'. There is evidence to suggest that Cheltenham looked towards late eighteenth- and early nineteenth-century London for architectural inspiration, as opposed to more obvious precedents such as Brighton, or the near contemporaneous Leamington Spa. This is suggested in the 1812 guidebook to Cheltenham, which observed: 'The houses are generally good, being for the most part either newly built or new-fronted; of the former, many are executed in the modern London style, with virandas and areas'. Indeed, this is the universal impression of Cheltenham – stucco and wrought-iron – but, in fact, prior to its Regency incarnation it was, as observed in 1812, 'built chiefly of brick'.

What was it about Cheltenham that created such fine architecture? The fact that it was fashionable for a period, thus creating the right ambience for distinguished architecture? Before the internal combustion engine, tarmac and concrete, Cheltenham, in certain parts, must have verged on the idyllic, which was to be found in the unostentatious. And so a halcyon rusticity can be detected in the 1783 guidebook for Cheltenham: 'Provisions in general are good here; the mutton peculiarly well flavoured, arising without doubt from the fine texture and sweet taste of the pasture on the hills.'

Again, something of the simple life can be detected in the following unpublished diary extract of the Hon. Anne Rushout, writing in October 1809: 'Go to Cheltenham . . . arrived about 5 o-clock and found a House ready for us in the High Street, my Brother tempted me to go to the Play to see Banister in Marplot.' Two days later: 'At 8 o-clock I walked to take a Glass of Water at the Old Well, then went on Mr. Thompson's walks, he has built a new Pump Room near the top of the field and a ride much further, on to the Bath Road . . . went to the Ball.' Formality was to creep in during the decade following Waterloo, when grander, more ostentatious, buildings were put up. A fully consolidated town can be found in *The Art-Union* for September 1846:

> CHELTENHAM has been for some years distinguished as the favourite abode of numerous wealthy families, and the resort of others seeking the renovation of health, by the use of its mineral waters. It has thus grown into a place of great extent and consequence, and become remarkable for the number of elegant buildings it contains.

A HISTORY OF MUTED PROTEST

One of the earliest coherent concerns about Cheltenham's architectural well-being came from Gerald Wellesley, later the Duke of Wellington, writing for *Country Life* in 1926. Wellesley warned in an understated and yet chillingly prophetic manner that:

The middle years of the nineteenth century saw the gradual decay of Cheltenham as a spa, and the Gothic revival and its concomitant tendencies in the realm of taste killed both the classical building tradition and all appreciation of its creations. Gloucestershire is now so proud of being the home of the romantic and *naif* Cotswold Manor House, that it has no place in its affectations for the demure and sophisticated architecture of Cheltenham. Most Cheltonians are only too apt to see little beauty in their town and to prefer the certainly delightful houses of earlier epochs. But 'there is one glory of the sun and another glory of the moon,' and if one likes Chaucer, one is not thereby prevented from liking Gray. At any rate, among architects an interest in the houses of the so-called Regency period is steadily growing. It is, therefore, very much to be hoped that the citizens of Cheltenham will develop, as those of Bath have done, a sense of their responsibilities as guardians of what is, perhaps, the completest neo-grec town in the country.

Let us waste no time in not being objective: Cheltenham is not full of architectural masterpieces. It might have only one, this being the Pittville Pump Room, but now we are becoming subjective. In 1945 the Georgian Group published an important report on Cheltenham. It is important for two reasons. It is probably the first expression of serious coherent concern about Cheltenham's heritage for the future, after Gerald Wellesley's prophetic warning in 1926. More importantly, so much of what was advocated in the report was to be ignored, or contradicted, over the next thirty years or thereabouts. Before the Second World War few had reason to be concerned about the future of Regency Cheltenham, with perhaps the exception of Wellesley's lonely voice in 1926: it was still very much intact. The only serious demolitions since Victorian times were the Cambray Pavilion, Bath Road, in 1929; Suffolk House in Suffolk Square, replaced by Eric Cole's incongruous (at least to their Regency neighbours) flats in 1935; Cambray House in Cambray Place in 1937; and the former Sherborne or Imperial Spa building on the Promenade in 1937. The Colonnade went in the early 1930s and the Cambray Spa in 1938, but the 'Regency' was still intact. It is arguable that the Georgian Group *Report on Cheltenham* achieved the right balance, when it reflected – and hence advocated – that:

There are certain types of buildings which deserve preservation, among them the building which is a work of art, and the building (or group of buildings) 'which possesses the routine virtues of the school of design which produced it.' Cheltenham possesses few of the former, but many of the latter, and it is these whose mutilation or destruction must be strenuously resisted.

Thirty years later Colin Amery and Dan Cruickshank chose to include Cheltenham as one of thirty desecrated British towns and cities in *The Rape of Britain* (1975). 1975 was an emphatic and somewhat panic-stricken year for architectural conservation – what with European Architectural Heritage Year; the foundation of SAVE Britain's Heritage; *The Rape of Britain*; Tony Aldous's *Goodbye, Britain?* and *The Destruction of the Country House, 1875–1974*, published the year before in 1974. A little earlier, in the 1960s, Nigel Temple, writing for *Country Life*, and Bryan Little, in *Cheltenham in*

Pictures, had both expressed grave concern about Cheltenham's future. Clearly, little had changed by the time of *The Rape of Britain*:

> The spacious elegance of Cheltenham is under threat of gradual erosion. Large villas are empty and derelict and the stucco fronts of the houses and terraces are crumbling and in need of constant maintenance. New developments are often too unresponsive to the nature of the town. A monolithic shopping development in the High Street [Tesco, etc.] already dwarfs its neighbours and introduces an ugly horizontal emphasis into a street of individual late-Georgian buildings. Several of the Regency villas near the centre have been converted into offices or hotels, while those in the outlying suburbs are being turned into flats. Ugly rear extensions and asphalt over the gardens are the unfortunate results of a policy that is transforming the garden setting into a scene of harsh bleakness.

And so between 1926 (Gerald Wellesley, *Country Life*) and 1995 (Timothy Mowl, *Cheltenham Betrayed*), we have a seventy year chronology of conservation writing with, arguably, little end result. One can very simply conclude that the impassioned advice of these not undistinguished writers, including John Betjeman in the 1950s, was simply ignored.

THE APPROACH

Cheltenham's Lost Heritage, as a project, has been ongoing since 1995. In 2000 I published a prequel of sorts in the form of 'Cheltenham Destroyed: an Introduction to the Lost Buildings' in *Gloucestershire History*, no. 14. As far as I am aware, the present publication is the first time that a collective account of the town's architectural losses has been published, and because of this *Cheltenham's Lost Heritage* is an attempt at a different approach to Cheltenham's history. Publications on Cheltenham are nowadays superabundant and can appear to be rather similar, treading on old and repetitive ground. *Cheltenham's Lost Heritage* might appear pessimistic and yet, it could be argued, the town still has a leading reputation for 'polite' architecture.

There is a creative, or at least investigative, aspect to the project in that I was once advised it would be impossible to find many pictures of destroyed Cheltenham; because the town lacks a comprehensive photographic archive – unlike somewhere such as Bristol, with its Reece Winstone Archive. Nevertheless, a prognosis such as this helped only to further my resolve in trying to locate pictures of elusive buildings. The amount of available information on any given building is always variable and in many cases it has been necessary to abridge severely, for the purposes of publication, what is known: but in others, such as Harley Lodge at Tivoli Circus (see pages 158–9), the facts presented here are about all that is known on the property in question.

Cheltenham's gradual erosion is graphically illustrated by the fact or statistic that of the 196 buildings illustrated in George Rowe's *Cheltenham Illustrated Guide* of 1845 only eighty-eight survive. In many cases all that remains to instruct us of a former house or villa is a stone or stucco boundary pier and a mature, albeit crumbling, brick wall – a situation perhaps akin to a discarded nut shell. Piers and walls can be found all over Cheltenham, where numerous gardens have been sacrificed to the car.

Following on from this general introduction, *Cheltenham's Lost Heritage* has been subdivided into the following chapters: public; spas; retail; hotels; ecclesiastical; and domestic.

CHELTENHAM'S DILEMMA AND THE PRESENT SITUATION

March 2002, and Edwardian Cheltenham was under threat with the demolition of what was a not unpleasant house, within a large garden, on the corner of Tivoli Road and Park Drive. Further Edwardiana has been eroded with the demolition of Gloscat's Christchurch Annexe, the former Central School for Advanced Instruction, on the Gloucester Road, which was built between 1906 and 1920. And still on the subject of Gloscat, there is surely one building of which no one – diehard Modernist or classical apologist – will be sorry to see the back of – this being the demolished Gloscat campus at The Park. Built sometime after 1955, it did much damage to the leafy integrity of The Park. In August 2002 Victorian Cheltenham was also under threat, with the demolition of a house on the corner of Gloucester and Lansdown Road. In other words, the threat continues. . . .

At the time of writing, Cheltenham development seems to be especially rampant, and there appears to be an alarming tendency to squeeze as many properties into a single plot as possible. Buildings are never, or at least rarely, pulled down for aesthetic reasons alone, but instead the usual motives seem to be those of vested interest and commercial gain.

Regency pastiche or pioneering Modernism – to choose from either presents a perpetual dilemma for a town such as Cheltenham. Admittedly, it has to be said that a book such as this almost inevitably concentrates on the town's 'polite' architecture and Cheltenham, like everywhere else, has considerable suburbs with their fair quota of dreary and ubiquitous architecture. Reams of protest have been published about Cheltenham's architectural plight, but let us nevertheless draw to a close with a slightly naive but none the less relevant letter addressed to the *Gloucestershire Echo* in November 1961, by an anonymous individual under the alias 'REGENCY-LOVER':

> Cheltenham is a unique town and our Regency buildings are some of the finest in England. Have we a right to destroy this heritage? And is it not a short-sighted policy? Visitors come from all parts of the world to see them, and if Cheltenham is reduced to a hodge-podge of buildings in all styles of architecture all charm and originality will be lost, and Cheltenham will sink to just another town. Surely the façade of the old houses at least could be preserved, and new buildings built in the Regency style.

Here follows a selection of the best of what has been destroyed. The general format throughout the book is for the historical illustration to be at the top of the page, and for a contemporary view of what is there now to be placed below it.

Oliver C. Bradbury, 2004

ACKNOWLEDGEMENTS

I am grateful primarily to Dr Steven Blake for passing this publishing opportunity on to me and for his help in arranging illustrations and commenting on the text. I am very grateful to Sir Howard Colvin for lending his name to my book by writing the foreword. Many others have also helped greatly such as Ken Pollock, who is something of a soulmate in this line of research, and the late Dr Nigel Temple for his photographic work and time; Isabel Armitage, Roger Beacham and colleagues at Cheltenham Library Local Studies Collection; David Bick; Christopher Bishop; Kath Boothman; Robin Brooks; Patrick Bryan; I.B.T. Caves; Amina Chatwin; Tony Davy; C.G. Diggins; Simon Fletcher, my commissioning editor at Sutton Publishing; Michelle Tilling; Andy Foyle; Mr and Mrs Halling; N.J. Hodgson; James Hodsdon; B. Hunter, M.A. Hyett; the late Phillip Jay; Jeremy Jefferies; J.M. Johnstone; M.A. Lockwood; C. Lowe; M. Lyon; H. Marshal; I. McKay; Dr Tim Mowl, Virginia Murray; Mary Nelson; Bonnie Nichol; C. Palmer; Tim Pearce; N. Rees; R. Rogers; Aylwin Sampson; P. Samuels; David Smith; Nicholas Kingsley, the County Archivist, and Paul Evans and staff at Gloucestershire Record Office; Isabel Syed; the Revd Brian Torode; Sally Trotman; A. Turner; H. Vowles; Christopher Wakeling; Bow Watkinson; Tricia Wilson; Dr Giles Worsley; and anyone else whom I might have inadvertently missed out. I am also grateful to Jean Badham of Badham Chemists Ltd for financial support, which I have used towards an illustration, and to the various individuals who have very kindly waived reproduction fees.

CHAPTER ONE
PUBLIC BUILDINGS

This chapter covers buildings which were neither private dwellings nor ecclesiastical. Cheltenham has lost many public buildings. These usually occupy prominent positions and so are focal points for any town. For this reason, their loss is more critical than that of private dwellings. Buildings from every aspect of public life have disappeared, including museums, asylums, banks, breweries, hotels, glasshouses, shops, markets, vicarages, clubs, schools, spas, libraries, parks, gardens, bandstands, pagodas and grottoes. Approximately sixty public buildings have gone.

The warning signs came as early as the 1860s, with the demolition of the Literary and Philosophical Institution on the Promenade. The following decade witnessed the destruction and the building over of Cheltenham's near sacrosanct Georgian genesis – the Old Well Walk. Here the Victorians showed scant regard for Cheltenham's rebirth as a spa town. No important buildings were lost but the Old Well Walk avenue, laid out as early as 1738–42, was clearly symbolic to the town. In 1900 the fine Regency Assembly Rooms by the architect Henry Kitchen were demolished to make way for the full-blooded Edwardian neo-Baroque of Lloyds Bank on the High Street. Kitchen's Assembly Rooms had in their turn replaced a short-lived building of the same purpose, possibly built by Henry Holland in 1784 and then rebuilt in 1809. Likewise, the original Montpellier Spa, dating from 1809, was replaced by George Allen Underwood's 'Long-Room' of 1817.

The original Pate's Grammar School, built as early as 1572, survived until 1887, when it was replaced with a Victorian Gothic pile (1887–9). Elizabethan Pate's is the greater loss as it was a rare example of pre-Regency Cheltenham, effectively from before the town was 'on the map'. Remarkably, Pate's, during the course of its long history, has gone through four 'incarnations': Pate's 'I' (1572); 'II' (1887); 'III' (1967) and 'IV' (1995).

Cheltenham has lost ten major hotels, eight of which had imposing neo-classical façades. The leading hotel was the ancient Plough. It was demolished in 1982. The present Regent Arcade façade bears a superficial resemblance to the Plough's Regency incarnation, as designed by George Allen Underwood (c. 1793–1829), a pupil of the distinguished architect Sir John Soane. The Plough's claim to fame was that its yard was 'one of the largest in the country'. A charming early nineteenth-century view of the yard – an unpromising subject – made by a guest survives in a sketchbook. It is labelled: 'Cheltenham Sep 5/15 The Coach Yard at the Plough . . . from my Chamber Window'.

Still on the topic of consumerism, Cheltenham, like most towns and cities, has lost almost all of its original shopfronts. None the less, an important survivor is the intriguing Art Nouveau shop fascia next to Cavendish House on the Promenade. In 1970 David Verey noted: 'Cavendish House has set a completely new trend in the Promenade, as have the new shopping blocks in Pittville Street and Winchcombe Street.' Cavendish House boasted the most imposing, and lengthiest, shopfront in Cheltenham. Evidence of Regency Cavendish House can still be divined in Regent Street. A few years ago I noted that a Regency Welsh dresser still survived in a basement stockroom at Cavendish House – an unusual survival in modern retail. A series of Regency shops called the Colonnade dating from as early as the 1790s – at the north end of the Promenade – were cleared in the early 1930s. All that remains of the Colonnade is Martin's, the county jewellers, incongruously clinging on to the end of the present sub-Art Deco apology. The greatest loss in this field is the eccentric neo-Hindu Market Arcade, which was built in 1822–3 on the site of the present Lower High Street Tesco supermarket and Bennington Street. Just how charming the Regency and Victorian shopfronts were can be gained by a perusal of early nineteenth-century guidebooks to the spa town.

Two of the greatest public building losses were George Allen Underwood's elegant Sherborne Spa, which survived in a debased form until 1937 before making way for a neo-Georgian cinema, in turn demolished in 1987, and the powerful, but short-lived, Greek Revival Literary and Philosophical Institution dating from 1835–6, designed by the stylistically eclectic Jearrad Brothers. Other unfortunate losses are the gem-like Mawe and Tatlow's Museum, once next to the present Montpellier Pump Room. It had been there for only twenty-six years when it was demolished in 1843. The Regency Albion Brewery on the Gloucester road went in 1876. The fine neo-classical façade of Gardner's Original Cheltenham Ale and Porter Brewery also went down with Victorian Pate's in the 1960s. Finally, the parks and open spaces at Jessop's Gardens, Montpellier and The Park have gone, been mutilated or are diminished. All three once featured dainty Chinoiserie pagodas, which have long since disappeared.

Opposite: **Montpellier Gardens**. The Montpellier pagoda was actually a bandstand and is the best known of the trio mentioned in the introduction above. It was first featured on the title page of Henry Davies's *The Stranger's Guide to Cheltenham and its Environs* (1832), where it was described thus: 'Immediately facing these conservatories is a light and elegant Chinese pagoda, erected by the present proprietors, Messrs. R.W. and C. Jearrad, and fitted up by them as an orchestra for the band.' The pagoda was presumably designed, as well as built, by the Jearrads in about 1830, when they laid out Montpellier Gardens after Papworth's more complex scheme of 1825–6 had been abandoned. Such a pagoda must be a late example of Chinoiserie, a style more associated with the eighteenth century than the 1830s. The pagoda thus represents the Jearrads' eclectic approach to Regency architecture, which entertained virtually all the known styles of the day – such as Christ Church's Gothic Revival, the Literary and Philosophical Institution's Greek Revival and the Italianate of Lansdown Court.

Pagoda,

Printed by Graf & Soret 14 Newman St

Jessop's Gardens. Jessop's Nursery Gardens were founded by Charles Hale Jessop as a commercial concern on a plot of land nearly 20 acres in extent and stretching from St James' Square down to the River Chelt. The Gardens were founded in about 1821–2, when Jessop married and moved into nearby St James' Villa. In 1845 the topographical artist George Rowe (1796–1864) described it thus: 'a well laid out Garden, with its Hot-houses, Green-houses, and Parterres . . . Aviaries, Pagodas, and Rustic Fowl-houses.' Elsewhere, 'Rustic work, garden seats, bee boxes, and gold and silver fish' could be found. The scene above, by George Rowe in 1836, can be compared to his description of a 'broad gravelled path leads through the gardens to the Bays Hill, crossing the river by a rustic bridge'. The Gardens were something of a menagerie too, with fancy breeds of rabbits, pheasants, fowl, owls and even a sea-eagle. Success was assured in the 1820s and '30s but by the 1840s Jessop was obliged to sell a fair amount of land to the forthcoming GWR, for their station which was to be built in St James' Square, and in 1855 disaster struck when the River Chelt burst its banks.

In 1858 Jessop was declared bankrupt and the Gardens were put up for auction. He died in the following year. The Gardens eventually closed for good in 1872, and by 1994 the site could be described as 'a waste of broken concrete, weeds and rubbish'.

Winter Garden, Imperial Square. Near despised by mid-twentieth-century writers, such as Sir Hugh Casson and Bryan Little, the Winter Garden was described by the former as 'hideous' and by the latter as a 'spacious, hideously glorified bird-cage'. Neither would have mourned its demolition, following a period of disrepair, in 1942. It was built in 1878–9 by the prolific and stylistically versatile local architect John Thomas Darby, and had brick walls and an iron and glass roof, which culminated in a dome nearly 100 feet high. The Winter Garden housed an ice skating rink and a large concert room. It has been described as 'Cheltenham's Crystal Palace', but perhaps a comparison with the nearer-in-date Alexandra Palace (1873) would be more apt.

Assembly Rooms, High Street. There were Assembly Rooms on the south side of the High Street from about 1734, but the first Rooms of any architectural significance appear to date from 1784 and have been attributed on stylistic grounds to the fashionable London architect Henry Holland. This building, above, known as the Lower Rooms, featured 'two public rooms where dancing and card parties alternated nightly throughout the Season'. In 1809 the Lower Rooms were rebuilt, particularly on the outside, and so it is not clear whether the above view of 1813 is depicting an elevation by Holland or a remodelled façade of 1809. The full rustication and door treatment would, however, point more towards the late eighteenth century than 1809 – when a smoother wall surfacing could be expected. In 1815–16 Mr J.D. Kelly rebuilt (though incorporating the 1809 works) new Rooms – at the staggering cost of £60,000 – to the designs of the architect Henry Kitchen; the High Street elevation is illustrated in the Cheltenham guidebook for 1816 (below). The Duke and Duchess of Wellington opened the rooms on 29 July 1816. The new interior was celebrated for 'the beauties of the ball-room with its fine floor, its great window and its eleven crystal chandeliers'. (The view opposite shows the 1816 interior in about 1825.) The Assembly Rooms were still used as 'a centre of fashionable engagements' up until 1900 and in that year it was to 'disappear for ever to make way for the new premises of its purchasers, Lloyds Bank'. Lloyds then proceeded to erect a somewhat ponderous neo-Baroque banking hall, to the designs of Waller and Son.

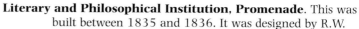

Literary and Philosophical Institution, Promenade. This was built between 1835 and 1836. It was designed by R.W. Jearrad in the Greek Revival style and demolished in 1860. It was described in 1840 as having 'a handsome classic portico, being an exact model of that of the Temple of Theseus'. The Temple of Theseus had first been introduced to this country, some seventy-seven years earlier, in the form of James 'Athenian' Stuart's garden temple at Hagley, Worcestershire, of 1758. The Literary and Philosophical Institution had a picture gallery – a feature that enables us to make a comparison with Lord Northwick's picture gallery building campaign at nearby Thirlestaine House. The late Jean Lacock, a local historian, has written: 'Lord Northwick paid a two-guinea subscription for 1839–40, when he was engaged in creating his picture gallery at Thirlestaine House, and was still a patron several years later.' Nevertheless, Northwick was not influenced – at least architecturally – by the Literary and Philosophical Institution picture gallery, which appears to have been designed not as a picture gallery *per se* but instead as a museum space. It had, architecturally and in terms of picture hanging, many Metropolitan overtones.

Mawe and Tatlow's Museum, Montpellier Walk. This was described in 1843, the year of its demolition, thus: 'a small oval building, called *The Museum*. . . . The claim of the latter to notice arises from the circumstance of its having been built by the celebrated mineralogist, Mr. J. Mawe, contemporary with the second Pump Room, erected by Mr. H. Thompson, in the year 1816–17. It is now used as a repository for the sale of curiosities and fancy goods.' It is not known who designed this attractive little building. Mawe and Tatlow's was demolished after only twenty-seven years of existence, possibly making it one of Cheltenham's shortest-lived buildings. Today's Barclays Bank was built on the freestanding site of Mawe and Tatlow's, next to the Montpellier Pump Room.

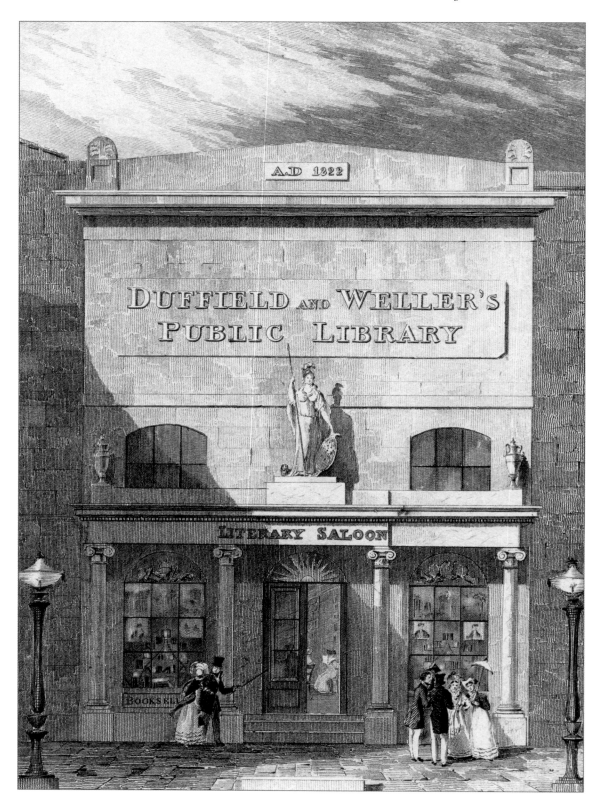

Duffield and Weller's, High Street. Perhaps the architect William Jay's first commission on returning to England in 1822 after a five year spell in South Carolina and Georgia, USA, was Duffield and Weller's Library on the High Street. It was built or remodelled in 1822, according to the date inscription on its pediment, and illustrated four years later in S.Y. Griffith's *New Historical Description of Cheltenham* (1826). Architecturally it bears several of Jay's hallmarks, but more important is the 'JAY. del' (not visible here) inscribed in the bottom left-hand corner of the façade elevation engraving opposite. Jay is not known to have drawn any Cheltenham buildings other than his own, and so this might suggest his authorship. Duffield and Weller's changed purpose many times, and was finally demolished in 1954.

Bettison's Library, High Street. The first library in Cheltenham was established in 1780, and by 1830 there were nine libraries. However, these were commercial circulating libraries – which remained the case until the public library was opened in 1889. Samuel Bettison, a bookseller, publisher and stationer, opened his library in 1817. In 1820 Bettison's was described thus: 'The Reading-Room, 80 feet in length, and supported by doric pillars, is terminated by a shrubbery, which tends to produce that serenity of mind so adapted to contemplation.' By 1824 Bettison's catalogue ran to 6,500 titles. The above library, as viewed in 1826, reveals – in an instant – the sheer elegance of Regency interiors. The dismissal of settees and pedestals to the walls is a typically Georgian touch. Bettison, aside from being a bookbinder and copper-plate printer, also offered 'Irish Scotch & French Snuffs' for sale. By 1957 this site was 152 High Street. It is not clear when Bettison's was demolished.

Lansdown Castle, Lansdown Road. The second of Cheltenham's 'castles' (the first being The Castle, Chapel Street, of *c.* 1814) was built in the 1850s, and is first marked on the 1855–7 Old Town Survey. It was a rectangular two-storey building occupying an irregularly shaped site between the Lansdown and Gloucester Roads. It had a three-bay façade, set behind a single-storey shopfront, and abutted a neighbouring house. The other two exposed elevations were only two bays wide. All the windows were mullioned and with hooded drip moulds. The parapet was battlemented and had projecting crenellated corner turrets on moulded bases. The overall construction was presumably brick covered in render. Originally a house near the tollgate, it later housed a grocer's in about 1870, and then a tobacconist's before demolition in about 1972. The castellated building lent its name to Gustav Holst's earliest known composition, the operetta *Lansdown Castle*.

The Albion Brewery, Gloucester Road, can be first seen on Bettison's *c.* 1819 map of Cheltenham. In 1826 Richard Masters and Co. ran the Albion as 'porter, ale, and table beer brewers'. Nearly twenty years later George Rowe commented on the 'old established *Albion Brewery*, which, for the supply of a good family beverage equal to home-brewed, has attained a celebrity as ancient as Cheltenham itself'. The site consisted of 'two acres and three quarters, with buildings thereon' and was valued at £2,500 in July 1873. At this date it was purchased by the Town Commissioners as a site for relocating the Cattle Market and Statute Fairs away from the High Street. The actual buildings were demolished in 1876.

The Upper Promenade. This terrace, opposite Cavendish House, was built in 1822, perhaps to the designs of George Allen Underwood. In 1823 Underwood designed the terrace, further along the Promenade, now housing the Municipal Offices and originally known as Harward's Buildings. The centre of the Upper Promenade terrace housed the Imperial Hotel (now Ottakar's), which was advertised as having just been built, in May 1822, by a portrait painter named Millett with 'the money earned by his talents'. Upper Promenade survives but its original balcony, perhaps Cheltenham's most idiosyncratic, has nearly all disappeared; it was intact, however, at the time of this photograph, taken in 1942. The slit above the paired columns on the far right (just visible here) is a device found in Sir John Soane's work, and in this case might suggest that his pupil Underwood worked here.

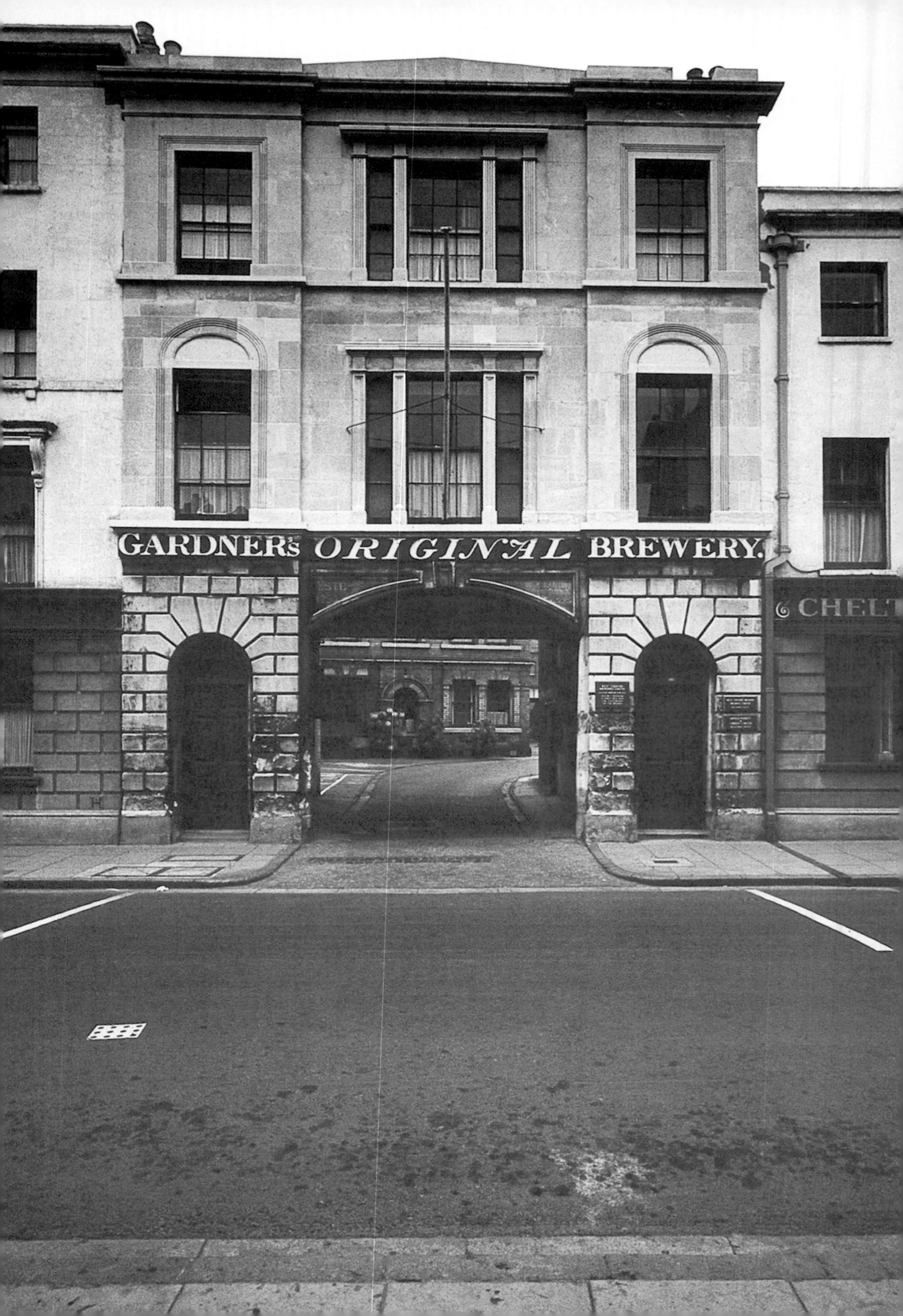
GARDNER's ORIGINAL BREWERY.
CHELT

Gardner's Original Cheltenham Ale and Porter Brewery, 160 Lower High Street. Gardner's Original Brewery was established in 1760 by J.T. Agg-Gardner, and the site was rebuilt in 1898, but during the intervening years the fine neo-classical façade, reproduced here, which once graced the High Street, must have been built before or during 1826, when it was included as a plate in S.Y. Griffith's *New Historical Description of Cheltenham* (1826). The plate, which bears little resemblance to the actual building, was drawn by the architect Edward Jenkins, but unfortunately we cannot therefore assume that he was the architect because he is known to have drawn other plates for the same publication. It was described in 1818 as being 'an excellent Porter and Beer Brewery, belonging to Mr. Gardner; which has long been established, with equal superiority and patronage'. Known as the Cheltenham Original Brewery from 1888, the site was partly cleared in 1967 and closed as a brewery in 1998. The view opposite was taken in 1960.

Market House, later Municipal Office, Lower High Street. The Market House was designed in 1808 by Edward Smith, a local architect, at the expense of Lord Sherborne. It was formally opened on 4 May 1809. The use of a Venetian window, such as the one deployed here, was an anachronism by the early nineteenth century. Bryan Little argued that the façade was a 'Palladian design that one might almost attribute to a period sixty years before its actual date'. By the 1840s the Market House had become the Public Office, where Cheltenham's administration, before it became a corporation, was based. During the twentieth century the building was used by Woolworth's and latterly by Tesco, before they moved across the road, adjacent to Bennington Street. The Market House was destroyed by fire and demolished in 1969. Curiously, all that survives of the Market House is a strip of ground-floor rustication, shown here, which clings on to The Famous, the outfitters, next door.

Pate's Grammar School, Lower High Street. The foundation stone for Richard Pate's new Grammar School, on the Lower High Street, was laid on 28 April 1572, and the building was completed in 1574. It was one of the few solid stone buildings within pre-Regency Cheltenham, and as such would not have looked out of place in a Cotswold town, such as Chipping Campden. Remarkably, Pate's was illustrated as early as 1586, at the head of an indenture now at Corpus Christi College, Oxford (see page 2). Although very much still a Tudor building, eighteenth-century Pate's had been given a slight makeover in the form of pedimented door cases for both entrances. There was a further addition in 1852.

By 1883 the old Grammar School had become too small and in 1887–9 it was replaced, after a competition, with a Tudor Gothic pile by local architects Messrs Knight and Chatters of The Colonnade, Cheltenham. It was actually designed by Knight, incorporating a combination of two of his designs. The builders were Messrs Collins and Godfrey, whose tender price was £6,270. Pate's 'Mark II' survived until 1967. Nevertheless, Elizabethan Pate's was the greater loss, as it was a rare example of pre-Regency Cheltenham. Neither Elizabethan nor Victorian Pate's was architecturally distinguished, but either would have been preferable to the Brutalist terrace which so blatantly planted itself on the Lower High Street in 1967. Most views of the Victorian school are oblique because of the High Street being so narrow; however, the view opposite, top, allows a broader view than usual. This photograph, from about 1890, shows a virtually brand new building, with a full complement of wrought-iron railings, which were removed during the Second World War. The plain Georgian building on the far left (demolished also in 1967) was – or was about to become – offices, with an associated remodelling, for the Cheltenham Original Brewery Co.

Lansdown station. Originally built as the Gloucester and Birmingham Railway station, the Lansdown railway station is one of several that Cheltenham once had. Built in 1840, it was opened in 1841, and designed by Messrs Daukes and Hamilton, architects to the Gloucester and Birmingham Railway Company. In 1961 Lansdown station lost its powerful early Victorian, late Greek Revival, Doric *porte-cochère* of nine bays, which was described in 1843 thus: 'Fronting the entrance gates, a neat colonnade is thrown out from the building, under cover of which the carriages and other vehicles set down their passengers.'

Lansdown station (continued). British Railways had a patchy record when it came to the conservation of important historic properties in their care, as was witnessed with the fate of Thomas Hope's The Deepdene, Surrey, and Euston station, London. Here, on the left, we see all that survives of Daukes's once splendid 1840 *porte-cochère*.

CHAPTER TWO
SPAS

When tasting the waters of Cheltenham in the twenty-first century it might seem almost incomprehensible to the modern man and woman as to how a town could have developed and prospered to such an extent on such seemingly foul-tasting mineral waters. However, there must have been nothing foul about these waters to a regular nineteenth-century visitor such as John Rushout, the second Lord Northwick. Witness Northwick's House Steward, Louis Mayland, writing to his master in June 1835: 'Henry informs me that you have no Cheltenham Watter [sic]. We have but Six bottle here if you Should wish to have Some Sent.' Northwick suffered from sometimes appalling bouts of gout, and so it is not surprising to note that he liked to have Cheltenham water always to hand. He eventually settled at Cheltenham in 1838, having been a visitor since about 1809.

There were at least twenty-six commercially operated mineral wells within Cheltenham itself. They date from about 1716, when the Original or Old Well was discovered, to a series of late wells not mentioned before 1944, this being the year of Edgar Morton's *Report on the Prospects of Developing the Mineral Water Wells within the Borough*. The Original or Old Well was the mother of all Cheltenham's wells. The exploitation of these wells for commercial gain, over two centuries, was the catalyst for a series of buildings, extant and demolished, ranging from the civic grandeur of Pittville Pump Room to what was in some cases little more than a garden shed housing a spring. The great days of Cheltenham as a spa were over by as early as 1850.

Gothic Cottage and the Octagon. These buildings were associated with a well, known as Octagon
Turret, which was once situated in a field on the site of the present Montpellier Street. The well was
opened in 1808. According to the 'Montpellier Wells' section in the *New Guide to Cheltenham* for 1820:
'In the lower corner of Montpellier field is a small octagon building, adjoining the Gothic cottage, which
contains three pumps, with the following waters, viz. *Chalybeated Saline*, pumped from a well 40 feet
deep, immediately under the building; *strong Chalybeated Saline*, brought by a pipe from a well under the

Gothic cottage, 55 feet deep; and *weak
Saline* water conveyed by a pipe from a
well . . . beyond the Gothic cottage. This
last has so little chemical impregnations,
that it has been denominated the milk
well. The waters of Bescroft-Meadow,
Octagon Turret, and Hygeia House are
chiefly used for making salts. . . .'

Gothic Cottage and Octagon Turret
were captured in pencil by an anonymous
hand in about 1810. The above scene
effortlessly captures the elegance of early
nineteenth-century Cheltenham. Note the
tented veranda with full-width overhead
balcony, and the unusual, slightly French,
roof dormers on the house on the right.
All three buildings, likely to have been on
the site of the present entrance to
Montpellier Walk, were probably
demolished when the shops of the Walk
were begun in 1843.

The Cambray Chalybeate Spa, Oriel/Rodney Road. The Cambray Spa was situated on the corner of Oriel and Rodney Road. It was built in 1834 for Baynham Jones, who lived at nearby Cambray House, and was demolished in 1938. It was designed by Thomas Fulljames of Gloucester (1808–74) and must be one of his earliest works, as he was only twenty-five when he designed it. It was designed in 1833 in a Tudor Gothic style, and it seems to represent something of a transition from a rather lightweight Georgian Gothic to a more serious and scholarly proto-Victorian Gothic Revival. Fortunately the complete working drawings – right down to the very last detail – survive in the Gloucestershire Record Office, and so it could conceivably be accurately re-erected. The spa was a compact octagonal building of two storeys, with a projecting entrance porch. The parapet hid a low pitched roof which met in the centre, with a cluster of Tudor chimney-stacks.

Also housed among the architect's drawings is a charming Greek Revival alternative design; it is, however, not as fully worked out as the Gothic scheme. It comprised a fluted Corinthian order on a high plinth and a deep, dentilled entablature below the parapet. The Grecian roof design is particularly engaging, with its rich mouldings which included leaf-shaped tiles and fleshy scrolls – all somewhat reminiscent of a lid to a fancy tea urn. Cambray's replacement is a scruffy section of hedgerow and the tarmac of a municipal car park.

Fowler's Chalybeate Spa, Cambray Place. J. Fowler's spa was established in 1807 at the south-west corner of Cambray Place. In 1834 it was superseded by the Cambray Spa, Oriel Road. Fowler's Cottage, as it was originally known, later became Woodlands, or Woodland Villa, and later still Woodlands Cottage, or 21 Rodney Road. It was demolished in 1973 and replaced by four modern houses known as Trelawn Court. At least one photograph exists of the above building in a semi-derelict condition. During the Victorian period the façade's symmetry was upset with the addition of a ground-floor bay window – executed in stone. Note the ramped gable ends, which are reflected in the extant, neighbouring Regency terrace in Cambray Place.

Imperial Fountain, Broad Walk. The above pavilion was built in 1826 in order to house an Italian marble fountain from Genoa, where it had been apparently looted by Napoleon's army. By 1826 the fountain had been acquired by Thomas Henney, developer of the adjacent Sherborne Spa. The pavilion, curiously described as 'a grotto-like building' in 1832 by the *Stranger's Guide to Cheltenham*, terminated a promenade once known as the Broad Walk, which was on the south side of Imperial Square. When the pavilion was demolished is not known, but the Broad Walk remained a strip of derelict land until as recently as 1995, when a neo-Regency terrace was built on the south side of Imperial Square. The fountain was removed from the pavilion in 1834, and after a long and chequered history it has been returned to near its original location, as a part of the recent development of the south side of the Square.

Sherborne Villa and House. The Cheltenham Hydropathic Institution occupied Sherborne Villa and House, which were once on either side of Sherborne Place. Sherborne House, on the right, was built in 1808, possibly by the Fairview developer and early Town Commissioner William Gyde (1780–1867). In December 1843 the soon-to-be-famous Alfred Tennyson, then living at 6 Belle Vue Place on the High Street, went into the Hydropathic Institution, staying there until spring 1844, suffering from a nervous complaint. He wrote to a friend: 'Of all the uncomfortable ways of living, sure an hydropathical is the worst: no reading by candlelight, no going near a fire, no tea, no coffee, perpetual wet sheet and cold bath and alternation from hot to cold.' The Institution operated until *c.* 1864 and the buildings were demolished in 1870 and 1882. This once sylvan site is now occupied by the less-than-sylvan George Bence and Sons, builders' merchants.

The Sherborne or Imperial Spa, Promenade. The Sherborne or Imperial Spa, as it later became known, was in a minor way one of Cheltenham's most important buildings – at least architecturally. In the first twenty years of the Sherborne's life as a spa it ranked with the Montpellier and Pittville spas. Following relocation in 1837, by the Jearrad Brothers, to the former ABC Cinema/Royscot House site, the Sherborne's fortunes were to be downhill all the way. The Sherborne Spa was demolished a century later in 1937 in order to make way for a neo-Georgian cinema, which in turn was replaced half a century later.

The Sherborne Spa was built in 1817 to the designs of George Allen Underwood, who was concurrently enjoying several other commissions in the town, such as Holy Trinity, the Montpellier Spa 'Long-Room' and the Masonic Hall. The Sherborne was originally situated on the Queens Hotel site, at the top of the Promenade. It has been suggested that the Promenade axis was possibly laid out at the same time by Underwood. The *Cheltenham Chronicle* recorded the spa's erection with numerous mentions and much excitement over the course of 1817–18. In 1845 George Rowe noted: 'this spa, with the fountain and shrubberies occupying the present *locale* of the Queen's Hotel, was in great repute; it, however, afterwards declined in public estimation, and gradually falling into disuse, the Pump Room in 1838 was taken down, and carefully removed.'

Although still elegant on its Promenade site, the spa building was in a debased and bastardised state – without its skyline statue and pedestal arrangement, neither of which were recreated. The best view of the exterior after the relocation is from a particularly graphic black and white 1892 photograph, reproduced here, which shows every detail with clarity. No longer used as a spa, it struggled on in a melancholy state as upholstery and cabinet showrooms during the Victorian period, and latterly as tearooms in the twentieth century, prior to demolition.

The Park Spa in fact started life as an entrance lodge to the Park Estate in Park Place. An 1833 'Plan of the Park Estate' reveals that the original intention had been to build two Greek Revival lodges, to the designs of Samuel Whitfield Daukes, on either side of the Park Place approach to the estate. At least one was in existence by 1837, when the 'North Entrance Lodge' served as the 'Park Estate Office'. Despite George Rowe's *Illustrated Cheltenham Guide* of 1845 mentioning lodges in the plural, the evidence – as suggested by maps and other sources – seems to imply that only one was ever built. Comparison of Daukes's 1833 design to the executed building, as depicted in various views, reveals that the lodge was loosely based on the architect's plans, with the omission of the more luxuriant ornamental detail.

The first mention of the relocated lodge as the Park Spa, is in the *Cheltenham Looker-On* for July 1850: 'immediately opposite the end of Park Place, to which site the little classical building, formerly used as a Lodge, near Segrave villas, has been removed and converted into a Pump Room. . . . The water was discovered some months ago. . .'. Quite when the Park Spa was demolished is not known; none the less, it probably lasted for only fifteen to twenty years. The Grecian temple was replaced by the Italianate Gonia, now Cornerways, which is estimated to have been built – once again perhaps by Daukes – in about 1865. All that remains of the temple is an entrance pier, formerly adjacent to the Park Place lodge, next to Segrave Villas (now Mercian Court). This completely overlooked pier, all that survives of Daukes's once monumental entrance to the Park Estate, tallies exactly with the 1833 design. We also know that one of Daukes's lampstand bases was built, albeit simplified in execution, if we compare a vignette of the locale in Rowe's *Guide* with the 1833 plan.

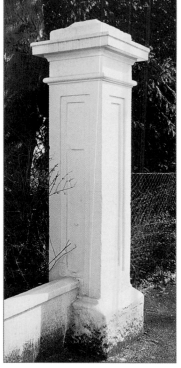

THE OLD WELL WALK.

The Old Well Walk was laid out in 1738–42, twenty years after a medicinal spring was discovered in a field south of the town. In 1818 it was described as a 'capacious, gravelled promenade, 20 feet wide, shaded by elms, whose aspiring tops shroud the avenue for upwards of 800 feet . . . occasionally, seats are placed for rest and conversation'. Like the Promenade, there are numerous views of the Old Well Walk, almost to the point of over-familiarity – at least to the Cheltonian. However, by 1890 the site had been gradually subsumed into Cheltenham Ladies' College. By this date 159 years of history had been completely erased. The above view, 'Drawn from Nature & on Stone', is by Henry Lamb and dates from about 1824–5.

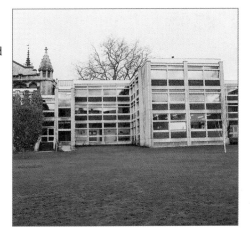

Old Well/Royal Well Pump Room. A building has
been on the site of the Old Well since 1738–42, when a
modest shelter was built over the well itself. The shelter
was a roofed canopy supported by four brick arches.
In 1776 William Skillicorne and a Londoner named
William Miller added the first of Cheltenham's 'Long
Rooms' to the well area. It was 60 feet long but narrow
in breadth and was to the east of the shelter. The view
opposite, top, commemorates the visit of George III to
Cheltenham in 1788.

In November 1848, after a period of decline in the
Spa's prosperity, the Old Well site was purchased jointly
by George Rowe and Samuel Onley. They swept away
all that remained of the eighteenth-century site. In
1849–50 Rowe and Onley built the Royal Well Pump
Room, which was to serve as a theatre, assembly hall
and music hall, as well as being a pump room.
The style was a ponderous Roman Corinthian.
Beyond the outer portico was a Corinthian pillared hall
(above) of 'undoubted dignity', according to Bryan
Little. It measured over 80 feet long and 55 across, and
had a painted backdrop depicting Lake Como. Success
was limited and so St Paul's College made use of the
room as an examination hall; it eventually closed in
1870. The Princess Hall of the Cheltenham Ladies'
College (opposite, bottom) was built on the site of
Royal Well Pump Room in 1895–7.

Montpellier Spa. As in the case of the original Montpellier Spa, one cannot always blame the twentieth century for continuous demolition. Montpellier Spa opened in May 1808 and was replaced by George Allen Underwood's 'Long-Room' of 1817. Could this be Cheltenham's most short-lived building? In 1812 Montpellier Spa was described by *Wood & Co.'s Improved Cheltenham Guide* thus: 'an elegant building, and a spacious pump-room, with a viranda in front, has been erected for the use of Subscribers'.

CHAPTER THREE
RETAIL PREMISES

Cheltenham has long been known for its shopping. George Rowe acknowledged this forte when writing in 1845: 'the Visitor will not fail to take in with a glance the busy scene which presents itself on either side of the spacious High Street. Its handsome shops, well stored with every variety of attractive merchandize – the broad pavements thronged with gaily-dressed pedestrians – and the road-way between, crowded with vehicles, from the coroneted equipage, down to the humblest trading conveyance.' It is, however, a pity that so few historic shopfronts survive – especially when one reflects upon the stifling blandness of modern retail.

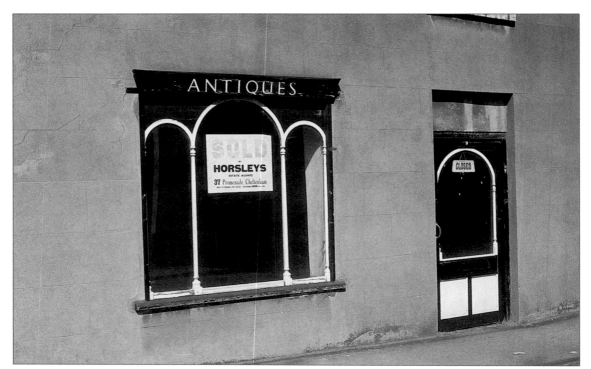

No. 9 St George's Place was a humble Victorian shop. Note the tripartite window with its quintessentially Victorian mouldings. Little is known about this shop but 5–9 St George's Place appear to have been demolished sometime before 1978, as part of a new shopping development linking with the High Street.

No. 11 Clarence Street. Clarence Street, named after the 1827 visit of Adelaide, Duchess of Clarence, was developed from 1827 to 1838. No. 11 is depicted (above) as an unremarkable vignette in George Rowe's *Illustrated Cheltenham Guide* (1845), where it was described thus: 'Messrs. King . . . is devoted to a branch of the "fine arts," very important in decorating the outward man. It has been said, and truly, that "clothes make the gentleman".' Messrs King was a tailor's shop. At some point, perhaps in the 1860s, half of no. 11's façade was rebuilt in a Ruskinian Gothic manner, which was in turn replaced by a modern shop fascia in the 1970s or 1980s. A more bizarre stylistic clash of Regency and Victorian, with so little compromise, is hard to envisage.

No. 33 Swindon Road. In 1606 this road was known as 'Swyndones waye'. No. 33 was one of several fine houses that once graced the now desecrated Swindon Road, The Elms being another. Little is known about no. 33, but it must have started life as a private dwelling in about 1820, but it appears to have been used as a business since at least Victorian times. In 1891–2 a William Green ran no. 33 as the Britannia Ale and Porter Stores. The elevation was somewhat unusual by Cheltenham standards. The main feature was the veranda, which lent the building an almost American Deep South quality. Amina Chatwin singled out the elevation's ironwork in *Cheltenham's Ornamental Ironwork*: 'Rustic simplicity and charm combined with elegance in the wrought ironwork of [this building] which stood, until 1973, opposite the top of St George's Street.' No. 33 and its immediate surroundings were replaced by the car park and amorphous building currently occupied by Matalan.

Cavendish House, Promenade. Originally known as Clark and Debenham, Cavendish House opened as a 'New Establishment' at 3 Promenade in 1826, selling 'a choice selection of Silks, Muslins, Shawls, Handkerchiefs, Gauzes, Ribands, Gloves, Lace, Hose and Fancy Articles of English and Foreign Manufacture'. Cavendish House, built sometime between 1820 and 1823, is a history of continuous expansion, involving the acquisition of neighbouring properties. The 1826 store was expanded in 1844 and 1851. By this date staff lived above the shop. In 1883 the Promenade frontage measured 142 feet in length and there were premises, originally a Regency terrace, used as workshops in Regent Street.

A further campaign was carried out in 1891, which included 'rich, massive, hand carved pillars of solid mahogany'. Cavendish House boasted the most imposing, and lengthiest, shopfront in Cheltenham: this can be clearly seen in the above photograph. The ornamental shop window clearly served as a unifying band, one which tied in a disparate row of properties behind an orderly frontage. Further extensions were made in 1903, 1920 and 1931, but by 1962 the store was in need of modernisation, which was carried out from 1962 to 1966, costing £800,000. This involved the demolition of the Promenade façade and all of the building directly behind it. The above view was taken in about 1960, when the historic shop's days were numbered. In 1970 David Verey noted of the new store: 'Recent developments in Cheltenham are frankly disturbing. Cavendish House has set a completely new trend in the Promenade. . . .'

No. 48 Promenade. When browsing through Regency and Victorian guidebooks to Cheltenham, one can see just how charming the shopfronts were, but as is the case in most towns they have been swept away, except for a precious few. No. 48 Promenade was one of the most charming. The Cheltenham Civic Society took a photograph of the shop before it was

demolished in 1931. Eighty-six years earlier George Rowe included a vignette of the shop in his *Cheltenham Illustrated Guide* of 1845. Rowe also indicates a precise location for the shop: 'Mr. MALPAS'S (*Chemist and Druggist*) Shop, late Mungeam, is nearly opposite the "Imperial," and just beyond the Imperial Library. It may be recognized by its chaste and elegant front, surmounted by a handsome lamp, with colored "bulls' eyes," which are probably meant as an extension of the display of the bottles of colored waters which usually adorn the chemist's window. The interior is fitted up in a tasteful manner, and is well furnished with the best and purest drugs and chemicals.' The shop was therefore probably where the Montpellier end of Cavendish House is now situated. No. 48 had clearly seen better days by the time the Civic Society documented the melancholy and empty shop, prior to demolition, when they noted: 'Now destroyed. Note the delicate Greek ornamentation.'

No. 346 High Street. In 1818, 346 High Street
was described as being 'next to the Ball Rooms' –
in other words the rebuilt Assembly Rooms of
1815–16. At this date it was the premises of
Wilson, a 'Hair Cutter and Dresser' and
'Ornamental Hair Manufacturer'. Wilson's
premises, on the High Street, were actually
separated from the Assembly Rooms by Rodney
Road. Thomas Wilson operated from several
premises, including a branch at 318 High Street.
Note the delightful and somewhat frivolous
Gothick fanlight glazing above the entrance.

No. 168 High Street. A rare survivor of pre-eighteenth-century Cheltenham, when the main thoroughfare had been a rough and ready muddy track, no. 168 was described in 1931, the year of the photograph on the left, thus: 'The last house of old Cheltenham before Regency times. Note the gables and stone tiles.' Estimated to be at least 400 years old in 1963, it had served time as a farmhouse, inn, 'music warehouse' and bakery. In 1805 it was opened as the first Government post office in Cheltenham and run by one Thomas Entwistle. In 1816 it became James Tinkler's basket, brush, sieve and rope shop. It survived as the Old Rope Shop until 1967, when it was demolished. No. 168 High Street was situated on the immediate left of the High Street entrance to the car park between Henrietta Street and St George's Street. It was a timber-framed building, with a long north-facing back range, and was fronted with a smaller range that faced the High Street. Nothing quite like it survives in Cheltenham, with the possible exception of Appletree Cottage on Haydon Road (below). In the 1840s George Rowe had noted 'an old gable-fronted house, a remain of Cheltenham's more primitive domestic architecture', which was situated also on the High Street 'Immediately opposite Cambray-place', but when it was demolished is not known. It can be seen on page 66.

The Market Arcade, High/Bennington Street. The best account of the former Market Arcade is to be found, some three years after it was built, in S.Y. Griffith's *New Historical Description of Cheltenham* (1826):

In 1823 the New Market House, built by Lord Sherborne, as lord of the manor, was opened. It is situated on the north side of the High-street, and is altogether on a scale admirably calculated to afford every requisite accommodation to the public. The building, which is 84 feet in length, and 42 feet in breadth, stands in the centre of a spacious square; the principal access to which is through the Arcade, containing, on the right side of the covered flagway, (an uncovered space being on the left for the market people, basket women, porters, &c.) a neat and very elegant range of shops, in which fancy goods are principally sold. Three portions of the square are appropriated to butchers' shops, constructed on a very convenient and airy plan. In the interior of the market-house, poultry, eggs, &c. are sold; and the ground in the rear is occupied by the stalls of green grocers, &c. This arrangement has given the highest satisfaction to all parties, concentrating the sale of all the necessaries of life, and removing from one of the principal promenades of this fashionable town, the great inconvenience of a public market, and the annoyance of petty stalls.

The Market Arcade was built in 1822–3, perhaps to the designs of Edward Jenkins – for he illustrated it in S.Y. Griffith's *New Historical Description of Cheltenham* (1826). Architecturally it was one of the most extraordinary buildings to have ever graced the town. Bryan Little described it thus: 'a bizarre composition of Gothic and "Oriental." I feel sure that [it] must have owed inspiration to the nearby Oriental-Gothic fantasy of Sezincote.' It was certainly unique to Cheltenham and yet curiously short lived. Only twenty-two years after it was erected George Rowe noted in his *Cheltenham Illustrated Guide* of 1845: 'It is rather remarkable, in a town so large as Cheltenham, that the market place should be so little frequented; but this arises, in great measure, from the number of good butchers, poulterers, and green-grocers' shops in nearly every part of the town.' Rowe's observation would go some way towards explaining why the market was demolished in the 1870s, only fifty years after it was built. The photograph opposite at the bottom of the page is taken from the *Cheltenham Chronicle and Gloucestershire Graphic* for September 1926, and is a reproduction of a print dating from the 1860s.

Opposite the Plough,

Gunton, Cook and Confectioner, High Street. A plate featuring Gunton was included in J.K. Griffith's *Cheltenham Guide* (1818). Gunton, situated opposite the Plough Hotel, sold 'Ice, Creams, Soups. &c'. Griffith noted, apropos Gunton, that: 'fashionable parties are supplied with dinners, ball-suppers, and all the *et cetera* of elegant entertainment'. Therefore Gunton was clearly an accessory to elegant living in Regency Cheltenham. By 1845 the premises appear to have been Mr Forget's: '*Basket Maker to Her Majesty*, whose beautiful specimens of basket-work, of "Osier's pliant twig," have been graciously received by his Royal Patron'. If apparently opposite the Plough, then just one aspect of the shop fascia might survive on either side of the present Thomas Cook (no. 159) and Barratts (no. 161); this being the quoins on either side of the shopfront in Griffith's 1818 view.

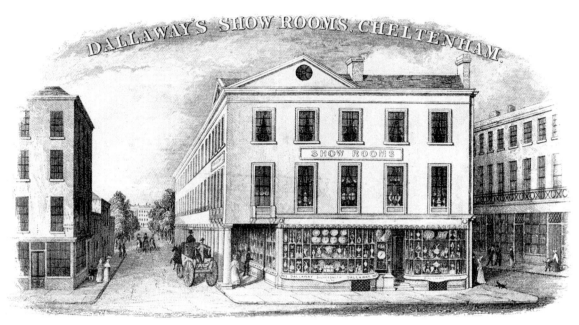

The Colonnade. This name originally referred to a building comprising a number of shops situated on the western side of the northern end of what is now the Promenade. The first stone was laid on 30 November 1791, making it an early Cheltenham development of the Regency period. By 1794 there were only six houses built out of a projected line of sixty-four, as had been envisaged in 1791, and it was still this length in 1817. A 1904 centennial publication by Charles Rainger claimed that his grandfather, Joseph Rainger, who had come to Cheltenham as a builder in 1804, was responsible for 'carrying out one of the early Street Improvements in the Town by setting back the frontage of the West side of the Colonnade, and constructing the existing Shops'. The removal of the Colonnade had begun as early as 1849 and not as late as 1937 – as has been previously understood. The Colonnade, as part demolished in November 1849, was situated on the north side of the street (now part of the Promenade) leading from the High Street into the Promenade proper. The last vestiges of the original Colonnade were finally demolished in 1882. The following, written in 1849, must surely refer to the above illustration, dating from 1841: 'the entire mass of building which rests upon it [the Colonnade], and projects ten or twelve feet into the street, will be brought down, and the houses thrown back to the Imperial Circus line of frontage'. Instructively, the 1849 account tells us that: 'The Colonnade was built thirty years ago, when this fancy in architecture was all the fashion.' Although such a date does not tally with 1791 it might suggest, nevertheless, a second phase of development of about 1819. There must have been further building after 1849, as there was a Victorian building at the north end of the Colonnade; its demolition was photographed in April 1937.

Haywood, Colonnade. The above photograph, taken in about 1883, is captioned: 'Looking up Colonnade toward High Street.' A delightful shopfront named Haywood, in the foreground, might well be by the Regency architect William Jay, for in February 1827 Jay put up a messuage, or dwelling house, in the Colonnade, Cheltenham, 'near Vincent House'. Unfortunately this is a vague topographical description; however, the 1820 Post Office map of Cheltenham does reveal a Vincent House in the vicinity of the Colonnade.

The stacked orders of Haywood's façade were unusual in that they begin comparatively high up in the order hierarchy – i.e. Corinthian, then Composite, as opposed to starting at the bottom with Doric followed by Ionic. Haywood's architectural features can be compared with other Cheltenham works by Jay, thus enabling an attribution.

CHAPTER FOUR
HOTELS

In 1783 it was noted that 'The Inns at Cheltenham are, the Plough, the Swan, the George, and the Fleece'. The late eighteenth and early nineteenth century was a time of considerable prosperity for Cheltenham's hotels, and this was owing to the influx of visitors to the spa. Captain Thomas Medwin, friend of Byron and Shelley, wrote to Jane Williams about his sojourn at Stiles Hotel in 1823:

I am living at a Pension – the oldest & largest in the place, which as far as the House, Table & accommodations go is excellent – & modest at 2 Guineas & a half a week. But Tables D'Hotes in England are exotic things, and do not suit John Bullishness & [?]. Abroad you meet foreigners of all nations & well informed and travelled people. Here – let me look round: 3 or 4 old maids on a forlorn hope – mere old [?Madams] that ought not to have been transplanted – an apothecary who bores me to death – & Sirs and Madames coming in every instant, with an Oh coming in every minute like a Bass note – & several nondescripts male & female, in the whole 14. One Aesculapius told me for my comfort that my liver was seriously affected & wanted to put me on a preparatory course of a month before I began swallowing the Water – but I began immediately – & this morning swallowed to his astonishment half a dozen [Rolls or Bowls: paper torn by seal] for breakfast.

As a spa, Cheltenham was in terminal decline by 1860. However, such a predicament must not be confused with the state of the town as a choice of residence, as the 1860s witnessed great domestic expansion. Hotel proprietors were among the first to bear the brunt of the spa's decline. A reflective *Cheltenham Looker-On* commented in May 1860: 'With the decline of Cheltenham, as a favourite watering place, the establishments adapted to that condition of existence have passed away, and given place to others of a more enduring character, because no longer dependant for their support upon the caprice of fashion, or the patronage of a few distinguished personages.'

The Plough Hotel, High Street, dating from at least 1654, was demolished in 1982 and replaced by the Regent Arcade, which retains a superficial facsimile of the hotel's façade. Historically, the Plough was the town's leading hotel for travellers from the seventeenth to nineteenth centuries, but after the Second World War it gradually declined in status. Up until a few years before 1826 it retained an early seventeenth-century appearance, but in tandem with the town's burgeoning prosperity the Plough was given a stylish neo-classical façade of seventeen bays across, which served to mask a much earlier building. This façade, somewhat in the style of Sir John Soane, is likely to have been executed by George Allen Underwood, architect of several other Cheltenham buildings at this period. According to George Rowe, in 1845: 'it has ever been identified with the early history of Cheltenham; from the humble country inn, it has risen through successive stages of improvement, keeping pace with the onward progress of the Town itself.' The Plough's 'immense yard [which] cannot fail to strike an observer' would eventually dictate the shape of today's Regent Arcade.

The Royal Hotel was situated on the site of the High Street entrance to the current Beechwood Shopping Centre. At ten bays wide, the Royal Hotel was a large establishment. The building that was demolished, presumably in the 1960s, was in existence by at least 1818, when it was described thus: 'situated in the most fashionable part of the High Street, nearly opposite the [Assembly] Rooms, within a short distance of the Theatre, and a pleasant walk of the different spas'. Like its rival, the Plough, the Royal Hotel had a large rear yard with livery stables running back as far as Albion Street. The Royal was splendidly engraved for S.Y. Griffith's *New Historical Description of Cheltenham* (1826), when it was under the management of Thomas Haines. At this period it had an extensive canopied balcony running across the whole façade, at first-floor level. The Victorians did away with the majority of the balcony, replacing its mid-section with an oriel window above the arched entrance. They also added, as an attempt to modulate the flat Regency façade, lintels, on consoles, above the ground and first-floor windows. As early as 1860 there were doubts about the Royal's sustainability: 'the Royal and the Belle Vue still remain hopefully holding their own against the surging tide of change, but whether successfully or not is impossible to say'. The view of the High Street (opposite, top) is by George Rowe and dates from about 1840; the photograph on the left was taken in 1957.

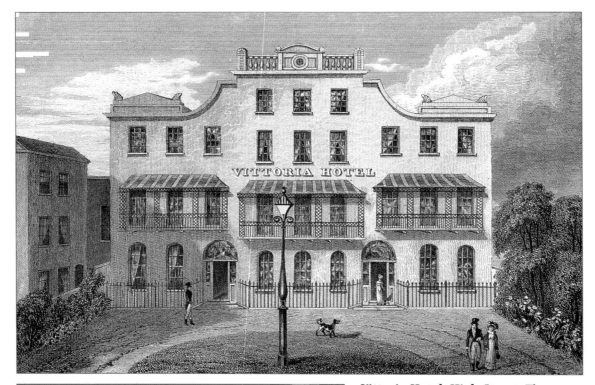

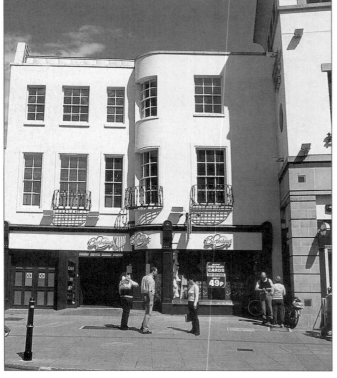

Vittoria Hotel, High Street. The Vittoria Hotel and Boarding House was situated opposite today's Lloyds Bank. In 1818 the Vittoria was described thus: 'This most elegant pile of building, forms a charming picture of architecture . . . and being about a hundred paces from the street, possesses the advantage of a lawn, shrubbery, and circuitous gravelled pathway to the hotel.' Sometime between 1818 and 1826 the Vittoria enjoyed a fashionable neo-classical facelift, turning what appears to have been a plain brick frontage into an urbane stucco essay, which would not have looked out of place in Regency London. Despite such a makeover, the hotel had closed as early as 1821. In 1860 it was noted that '*The Looker-On* is old enough to remember the Vittoria Hotel, one of the first of these establishments which ceased to be self-supporting, and which was converted into private dwelling houses at least a quarter of a century ago.' Until very recently the last vestige of the 'hundred paces from the street' survived as the deep indentation (now partially filled) of the two shops next to the Beechwood Shopping Centre.

George Hotel, High Street. George Rowe's
view of the High Street in 1840 depicts
Cheltenham at its most confident. It would
appear that every single building in this view
has been demolished. Note the diminutive
figure in the centre foreground: it is possibly
John Millbank, the dwarf muffin seller, who
was only 3 feet 8 inches tall. The George
Hotel, later an Auction Mart and
Pantechnicon, was described by Rowe in
1845: 'may be readily recognized by its
handsome portico covering the approach to
the house, and affording a convenient
protection on alighting or entering carriages
or public conveyances. This house is fitted
with every elegant and necessary
convenience, for the reception of Private
Families and Visitors, under the careful
superintendence of Mr. FLEISCHMANN.'
The George Hotel, formerly the George Inn,
had been one of the town's principal inns
since the 1740s. In 1818 it was considered
thus: 'co-equal in every respect to the
Plough. In addition to the Hotel, are very
extensive Wine and Brandy Vaults.' The two
trades often went together at this period.
By 1906 the balcony and *porte-cochère* had
gone to reveal a surprisingly flat, but still
elegant, stuccoed neo-classical elevation.
The Auction Mart and Pantechnicon, which
had opened in 1860, was demolished in
order to make way for Marks & Spencer.

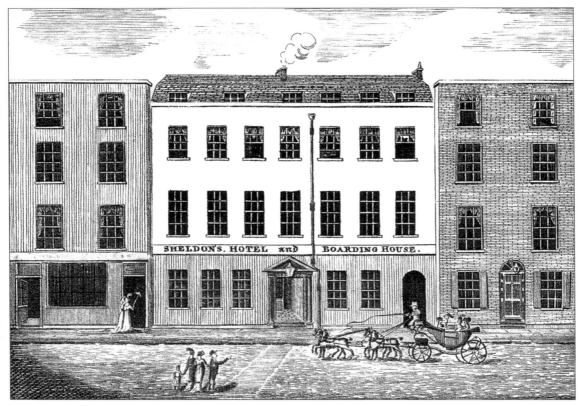

SHELDON'S HOTEL and BOARDING HOUSE.

The York Hotel, High Street, in existence
by at least 1800, was one of the principal inns of the
coaching era. By 1818 it was known as Sheldon's.
J.K. Griffith's *A General Cheltenham Guide* (1818)
informs us that 'The complete revision the house
has undergone in improvement, furniture, &c. has
given it features of domestic comfort and elegance.'
The façade was seven bays wide and almost
without any ornament. The site is now occupied
by 85 High Street.

Fleece Hotel, Lower High Street. In existence by at least 1783, the Fleece was a large Lower High Street 'Family and Commercial Hotel'. The hotel, at eight bays in width, was an exceptionally broad building. In 1826, as seen in S.Y. Griffith's *New Historical Description of Cheltenham*, the Fleece was a very plain Regency building, with little more than its fenestration for decoration. Its final appearance, however, appears to have been early to mid-Victorian in style (and date), suggesting that the Regency building had been simply too plain for Victorian taste. Although still plain, the remodelled Fleece had good detailing in the form of ground floor rustication, an arched side entrance, quoins, first-floor window lintels on enriched consoles, and – above all – the splendid establishment plaques. The Fleece's High Street elevation worked successfully with its neo-classical neighbour, Gardner's Original Cheltenham Ale and Porter Brewery. In 1826 the Fleece's proprietor was a Thomas Hurlston, a 'Wine & Brandy Merchant', who also offered 'Post Chaises & c'. Since 1823 the Town Commissioners had met monthly in a back room provided at the Fleece. The hotel was demolished along with the rest of the north side of the Lower High Street, between Bennington and Henrietta Street, in 1967 – a particularly unfortunate year for Cheltenham buildings.

Hotel Majestic, Park Place/Ashford Road. The Majestic could well be included in the domestic chapter of *Cheltenham's Lost Heritage*, having been originally built as a private house on the Park estate. Before opening as a hotel in May 1932 it was known as Nethermuir. Quite when Nethermuir – presumably a Victorian change of name – was built is difficult to determine; however, the building appears to be on W. Croome's 'Plan of Leckhampton Parish' of 1837. It is not on H.S. Merrett's *This Plan of the Town of Cheltenham, and its Vicinity* of 1834, which suggests that the house was built sometime between 1834 and 1837. According to the *Cheltenham Chronicle*, at the time of the Majestic's opening 'the position and construction of the house made it eminently suitable for conversion to residential hotel purposes'. The *Chronicle* featured photographs of the exterior, lounge, dining room and opening ceremony. In 1935 the Majestic was 'greatly enlarged' to include, by now, forty-eight bedrooms. Architecturally, Nethermuir shared much in common with the other large houses of The Park. It has been replaced by the Park Gate development. The Majestic later became the Park Place Hotel, which burnt down in the late 1980s.

CHAPTER FIVE
ECCLESIASTICAL BUILDINGS

Fortunately the destruction of the majority of Cheltenham's churches and chapels has been avoided. The sheer quantity – and variety – of ecclesiastical buildings in the town can be appreciated when studying Steven Blake's *Cheltenham's Churches and Chapels* (1979). It is now almost forgotten how much of a religious centre Cheltenham had become during the Victorian period, following on from the comparatively frivolous Regency heyday. The most important loss, although now hardly remembered, was J.B. Papworth's St John's, Berkeley Street, in 1967. Unfortunately the Victorians had already altered the church beyond recognition into a somewhat bland Gothic affair between 1867 and 1872. Any Greek Revival church, as it was originally built in 1827–9 by Papworth, would have been by example a great asset to the town. Other losses have been Samuel Onley's, albeit somewhat ungainly, Congregational church once on the site of the Winchcombe Street Odeon. It was demolished in 1932.

The late Italianate Royal Well chapel was demolished in the mid-1960s in order to make way for a car park behind Royscot House. St Philip's, Leckhampton, by the Cheltenham-born architect Edwin Hugh Shellard (1815–85), and the neo-classical Roman Catholic chapel in St James' Square were both short-lived, and in time were replaced by worthy, but none the less dull Victorian churches in High Gothic style.

St John's, Berkeley Street. It is a pity that John B. Papworth's sole Cheltenham church (aside from completing someone else's work at St James', Suffolk Square) has been demolished. However, it was never very popular – at least architecturally. George Rowe noted in 1845: 'St. John's is a plain and substantial structure, possessing few claims to exterior architectural beauty; but is very tastefully fitted up interiorly, and is calculated to accommodate about 800 persons.' And Bryan Little over a century later (1952): 'It seems never to have been a church of much distinction and was rebuilt in Victorian Gothic.'

St John's was built between 1827 and 1829 in the ubiquitous Greek Revival manner of the period. The only other extant Greek Revival church in Cheltenham is John Forbes's St Paul's. Admittedly Papworth's architectural composition was somewhat ungainly, but nevertheless rather more engaging than Charles Martin Müller's (an architect, based at Ormond Terrace, Cheltenham) bland Gothic remodelling of 1867–72 (opposite, top), when all the former's work was destroyed. St John's cupola clearly illustrates the recurrent British problem of marrying the traditional west end tower on to a Greek or Roman temple format. One might assume that an architect of Papworth's ability could have resolved such a problem, but many of the leading neo-classical architects, such as Sir John Soane, struggled with this peculiarly British problem.

Little is known about Papworth's interior – save for the comprehensive set of designs housed at RIBA, London. David Verey described the Victorian interior as having: 'a large galleried auditorium, with an extraordinary trefoil-shaped ceiling of enormous span, having wood panels overlaid with fretwork, with perforated zinc plates for ventilation, and a lovely dripping valance, barge-board style, on the E wall'. Owing to a dwindling congregation the church was declared redundant in 1967 and demolished in December of that year. St John's legacy is now a plot of grass, a road widening and a house opposite, named St John's Villa.

First Salem chapel (Old Town Hall), Regent Street. Originally a riding school but always ecclesiastical in aspect, this building became the First Salem chapel between 1835 and 1844, when it was closed. First Salem then became a venue for public meetings, travelling shows and other entertainments. It finished its days as the 'Old Town Hall' storeroom for Cavendish House and was eventually demolished in 1982. The Old Town Hall was a plain brick building, with a broad pitched roof and gabled ends. The south end was the principal elevation, with an attractive first-floor segmental arched window, which had Gothic glazing. The north end, by comparison, was very plain; the elevation was composed of three pointed arch windows – one of which still had delicate Gothic glazing until the late 1970s.

St Philip's Church. St Philip's, Leckhampton, was built between 1838 and 1840 in what was effectively still a Regency Gothic style, which survived into the early Victorian period. Bryan Little described the church thus: 'no more than an unexciting attempt at the "Early English" that the thirteenth century had favoured'. It was designed by E.H. Shellard. In 1843 St Philip's was described as being 'neat in its external appearance, and has a very pretty little tower, eighty-six feet in height, rising above the eastern entrance'. In 1879 the church was demolished and replaced by the larger St Philip and St James, which exists to this day.

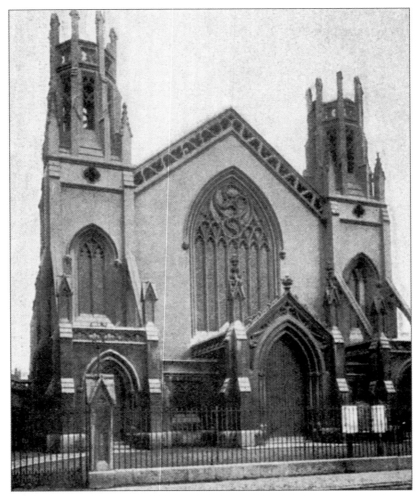

Highbury Congregational church, Winchcombe Street. The Highbury Congregational church, seen here in the *Cheltenham Chronicle and Gloucestershire Graphic* for January 1932, 'was built to re-house the congregation meeting at the former Snow's Chapel [Grosvenor Street] from 1827 onwards. A large, roomy building, designed by a local architect, Samuel Onley, Jnr., in the Gothic Revival style, it was closed in 1932 when the congregation moved once more to the present Highbury Chapel in Priory Terrace. The chapel was later demolished, and its site is now occupied by the Odeon Cinema.'

The church was built in 1850–2 and first illustrated in Goding's *History of Cheltenham* (1853). Onley's chapel was a curious looking building and somewhat clumsy in terms of composition, but none the less not without some interest. The façade was crammed full of devices, for example flying buttresses, crocheted pinnacles and perforated tracery. Perhaps the most peculiar features were the little turrets on either side of the main gable, which were open to the elements, and the trio of projecting porches with their flying buttresses supporting the twin towers. The chapel was considerably less than a hundred years old at the time of demolition, but such an emphatically Victorian building must have been deeply unfashionable by the 1930s. Highbury's replacement with a cinema must surely represent the ultimate triumph of pleasure over religion in a less moralistic century.

At least one view of the interior exists, this being a 1906 postcard which shows a simpler than expected interior consisting of collegiate-style aisled galleries. The dominant feature was the central organ behind the pulpit, housed in a large ogee-shaped arched recess.

Royal Well chapel. The foundation stone for Royal Well chapel, once situated at the bottom of the Old Well Walk, was laid on 24 June 1864. This Methodist chapel was opened for worship in March 1866. At this time it was described as being 'in the Corinthian style of architecture, and is 75ft. long by 59ft. wide. The front elevation has a noble and imposing appearance.' The ground floor included a spacious lecture hall, vestries and an apartment for the chapel keeper. The body and galleries of the chapel were approached by staircases situated on either side. The galleries ran all around and were 'supported by bronzed columns, surmounted with massive carved capitals'. The chapel was designed by C.M. Müller, an architect active between 1868 and 1900 according to RIBA records, and so the Royal Well chapel must represent one of his earliest works. The chapel is a good example of an Italianate alternative to the popular Gothic of the period. It was converted to a garage in 1936 and subsequently demolished in the mid-1960s.

Walker Memorial church, Whaddon Road. The Walker Memorial church was built and opened at the expense of the Revd James Walker, a minister of the Church of Scotland, in 1877. Services, following the rites of the Church of Scotland Communion, were held here until Walker's death in 1911. Architecturally crude and constructed of corrugated iron, Walker's church nevertheless had some naïve charm, as can be seen in the basic window tracery and gables. It had much in common with, and was perhaps based on, the temporary church in Clarence Street of 1859 (also realised in corrugated iron) which housed the displaced worshippers of St Mary's, the parish church, during the latter's restoration of 1859–61. The Walker was later known as the Cheltenham Evangelical Free church, and was demolished in the late 1980s. A new church has been built behind the present flats on Whaddon Road.

New Burial Ground memorial vault. This funeral monument has been well covered by the local press over the years, beginning with the *Cheltenham Chronicle* on 31 October 1861: 'A MONSTER VAULT is being erected in the Cemetery, by Mr. Darby, the cost of which, we hear, will be nearly £1,000. It will be 12 feet in depth, and over it will be erected a large room, having a window towards Bays-hill, and a large doorway facing High-street. The walls are about nine feet high, and are of carved stone, and the figure of a dog, cut in stone, will be placed over the building. The cost of the carving alone has been upwards of £100, and the vault when completed will, no doubt, form one of the most striking objects in the Cemetery.'

The 'Mr. Darby' must be the architect John Thomas Darby, who was responsible for the Winter Garden and other local works. There were further articles on the vault in 1908 and 1936. In 1936 the *Cheltenham Circular* published a letter to the editor by a W.L. Brown, which stated: 'The tomb was built by my grandfather, John Brown, for a gentleman who was a great dog-lover, and who intended his pet to find a last resting place in the family vault. It was pointed out to him, however, that this was contrary to the rules of the Church, and he then decided that a carving of the dog should be made and placed on the tomb. Shortly after the work was completed, the dog died, and his owner in great grief departed for Italy, where all trace of him was lost.' The 1908 article carries an excellent photograph, above, of the vault flanked by two men, allowing us a sense of scale. Note the unusual positioning of the two inverted carved stone torches. This bizarre burial vault would not look out of place in Highgate Cemetery, London, but was clearly unparalleled in Cheltenham. Unfortunately it was demolished when the former St Mary's Cemetery was razed for the Churchill Memorial Gardens in 1965.

CHAPTER SIX
HOUSES

The domestic chapter of this book, the largest section, is an introduction to the demolished private dwellings of Cheltenham. At least sixty free-standing houses or villas have been demolished, at a conservative estimate. Terraces, being more commonplace, have generally been excluded from the survey.

A modern infill, within a row or terrace of Regency or Victorian houses, is a sure sign that there was once a building contemporaneous to its neighbours. A good example would be the unsightly replacement of Bayshill Lawn on Parabola Road by Brian Tait, in 1960. Historic maps, such as H.S. Merrett's *This Plan of the Town of Cheltenham, and its Vicinity* of 1834 and the detailed OS maps of the 1880s, are invaluable in determining the existence of long-forgotten demolished buildings.

Demolitions such as The Priory on the London Road in 1967 and Cambray House, in Cambray Place, are particular for at least two reasons. They were both architecturally distinguished, although their architects have never been identified. Their scale was imposing by Cheltenham standards, but more importantly their undistinguished replacements have deprived the immediate locality of an authentic focal point within the surrounding architectural hierarchy. Cambray House was once the focal point, terminating Cambray Place's long vista from the High Street. The Priory's unsightly replacement did little to relate to its polite Regency neighbours. Ironically this 1968 replacement would eventually go full circle; twenty-five years after it was built it was empty, self-defeated and derelict. In 1998 it too was demolished. The exterior of the original Priory has been loosely re-created to house 'just 32' flats and an underground car park. The Priory was Cheltenham's domestic masterpiece and arguably the single most important house to have gone.

Other demolitions included Tudor Lodge at The Park by the Victorian architect S.W. Daukes, and perhaps John Middleton's domestic masterpiece, Abbeyholme, in the Overton Park area, both in the Gothic Revival style. Abbeyholme was important for its pre-Raphaelite overtones and sumptuous, rich and ornate Victorian detailing. It was possibly the only house in Cheltenham ever to have been designed by an architect for himself – in this case John Middleton. Two houses by an architect of national importance were J.B. Papworth's Rosehill, though already heavily Victorianised by Waller and Fulljames, on the Evesham Road, and 1 Lansdown Crescent, now replaced in facsimile. Why Rosehill was allowed to be demolished, as recently as 1991, is a mystery; surely the later outliers could have been removed and the grounds executed in accordance with Papworth's plans, housed at the RIBA, London.

A minor but unique demolition was The Rock House, once enhancing Vittoria Walk. It was the only building in the town covered in chocolate coloured rock, fish-scale roof tiles and with an internal grotto. Although predominantly a neo-classical town, Cheltenham could also boast a domestic grotto, which is indicative of the diversity and fertility of its early Victorian period.

The list goes on. Bays Hill Lodge, where George III stayed on his seminal 1788 visit to the developing spa town, was, admittedly, not badly replaced in Victorian times. It is a well-worn cliché that the Victorians showed disdain towards the creations of the eighteenth century, and one can find numerous examples to illustrate this point, but the opposite can also be argued. Still on Bays Hill Lodge, the *Cheltenham Looker-On* reflected, somewhat nostalgically, that 'this architectural curiosity which so remarkably linked the present with the past in the history of Cheltenham, will be effectually cleared away, and leave behind it an existence only in the memories of old inhabitants'.

Let us not forget Grove Cottage, even though it is not featured in this publication. It was a 'picturesque building at the end of the Royal Well Walk', which was demolished in 1844. Its significance was that it 'was one of the first of the mansions built in Cheltenham upon the discovery of its mineral springs, and was, at least, co-eval with Bays Hill Lodge . . . [which is] now the only building on the Bays Hill Estate – the Pump Room and Well House excepted – dating its erection in the last century'. Such a sentiment illustrates how, contrary perhaps to what we might believe now, even under the Victorians nothing stood still: progress was continuous.

The loss of the exquisite Portland Tabernacle on Portland Street in about 1980, built as a private dwelling in 1818 and converted to religious use in the late nineteenth century, is unfortunate as it was one of the few Cheltenham buildings from the Soanean school, and perhaps by Sir John Soane's pupil, George Allen Underwood. Fortunately its visual counterpart, the Masonic Hall, survives.

Eye, Ear and Throat Free Hospital, North Place. This building has been included in the domestic section as it must have started life as a private house. The double-bow elevation seen in the above 1908 illustration can be clearly divined in H.S. Merrett's *This Plan of the Town of Cheltenham, and its Vicinity* of 1834; nevertheless the building would appear to date from about 1820. A wing to the south of the bowed elevation was added in 1908 and later, perhaps in the 1930s, so raised that the furthermost Regency bow had been destroyed, or totally subsumed into the south wing.

Camden Terrace consisted of three houses situated in a lane between North Place and Portland Street. The terrace first appears, unnamed, on H.S. Merrett's *This Plan of the Town of Cheltenham, and its Vicinity* of 1834. The terrace must have been demolished, with much else of North Place and Portland Street, in the 1960s in order to make way for the now unsightly Portland Street car park. Architecturally the terrace was a halfway house between the humble artisan housing of Fairview and the comfortable villa, or grand terrace, of bourgeois nineteenth-century Cheltenham. Camden Terrace had ground-floor verandas, softening the transition between house and garden. This subtle arrangement cast attractive

shadows on the stucco façade – an ambience so quintessentially Regency and peculiar to Cheltenham, with its superabundance of ornamental ironwork.

Camden Terrace was an instructive example of how charming fairly standard, and somewhat formulaic, Regency housing could be. It can be compared to terraces in London Road and Prestbury Road.

No. 14 North Place. This pathetic picture, taken by Dr Steven Blake in about 1979, shows 14 North Place clinging on to life, before its eventual demolition in about 1980. In 1968 no. 14, then occupied by a Mr and Mrs H.W. Haines, was excluded from the compulsory purchase order that had been so drastically implemented on the rest of the terrace. An unnamed and undeveloped plotline for what was to become North Place is marked on an 1806–10 map of Cheltenham. However, by 1819 North Place had been built up.

Nos 31 and 32 North Place. These two houses were probably built by about 1819. The photograph on the left was taken by the Cheltenham Civic Society in 1931 and reflects the depressed, un-gentrified nature of Cheltenham between the wars. The melancholy reflection on the fanlight's mottled glass and the well-worn steps speak volumes. It also shows how much decorative ironwork could be contained in a comparatively small space: note, too, the ornamental foot scrapers. Little else is known about these two forlorn properties; save to say that the terrace they belonged to was demolished probably in the 1960s.

Old Farm, St George's Place. Old Farm was in existence by at least the 1740s. Once a home of the Masons, then the Skillicornes, developers of the first spa, by 1837 it was listed as 'Old Farm, 38, St. George's Place'. In 1857 it was advertised for sale as 'a genteel VILLA RESIDENCE. . . . Containing Four Sitting Rooms, Four Best Bed Rooms, Servants' Apartments . . . Pleasure and Kitchen Gardens, with about Two Acres of Land'. Unfortunately demolition followed in 1858, and so the stereoscopic view (right) must therefore be a very early photograph. The site was built over in 1869 with St Mary's Hall, the Female Training College, later known as Shaftesbury Hall and now part of the Chelsea Court residential development.

In the eighteenth century Old Farm was a modest self-contained farmstead, but by the nineteenth century, as can be seen here, it had been given a Gothick Revival makeover. This included a distinctive ogee arch over a door, deep eaves and bargeboards, enormous chimney-stacks, pinnacles and pendants. The large garden was attractively laid out with a carriage sweep.

Entrance to Bays Hill.
In St George's Road is one of
Cheltenham's grandest terraces –
Bayshill Terrace. This terrace,
built in 1838–40, would not have
looked out of place in Nash's
Regent's Park; however, the
twentieth century witnessed the
demolition of two of its porticos.
George Rowe noted in 1845 that
'the umbrageous Elms of the Old
Well Walk are seen towering
above the massy pillars, which
stand at the entrance to this
beautiful locality'. The pillars
must have been swept away with
the development of the Ladies'
College from 1873 onwards.
In August 1908 it had been
proposed that 'The Houses in
Bayshill Terrace, Cheltenham . . .
should be converted into
Municipal Offices.'

The Priory, London Road. In 1961 Gwen Hart swiftly demolished the apocryphal local myth that the Regency house known as The Priory stood on the site of an eighth-century priory. Hart wrote: 'It may be stated at once that there is no connection between this Regency building and the ancient Priory known to have existed in the town in the eighth century.' Nevertheless, The Priory's origins can be traced back to at least 1781, when it was known as The Cottage. An 1824 Cheltenham Manor Court Book provides the link between these two properties: 'Mansion House heretofore called the Cottage but now commonly called or known by the name of the Priory'.

However, The Priory we knew, at least architecturally, was an early nineteenth-century building and not a late eighteenth-century creation. The most informative account of The Priory is from a sale particular in the *Cheltenham Journal* dating from 20 October 1828. Here it is described thus: 'All that CAPITAL MESSUAGE or MANSION HOUSE, called "THE PRIORY" late the residence of Charles Henry Marshall, Esq. with the PLEASURE GROUND adjoining. This MANSION has been erected within the last three years in the most substantial manner. . . . The elevation of the House is of a most commanding description, is fronted with stone, and forms a very elegant feature on the entrance to Cheltenham by the London road.'

The most curious and illuminating point to emerge from this description is that 'This MANSION has been erected within the last three years'. This would suggest therefore that the house was built in 1825. Architecturally, 1825 would be an acceptable date for The Priory, but there is a conundrum in that the building is unambiguously depicted on the 1820 Cheltenham map. The Priory might also be on Bettison's *c*. 1819 map of Cheltenham, but the 1820 is the first secure topographical depiction, where it is indexed 'Priory'. The 1820–25 dating might simply be explained by the fact that the house perhaps took five years to complete, but this is of course merely conjectural. If it was not built for Charles Henry Marshall, he (as Cheltenham's Master of Ceremonies) was at least an early occupant in the 1820s. In September 1827 Marshall hosted a ball at The Priory, where 'by the opening of Seven Large Rooms, his Friends and the Public will find ample accommodation'. An indicator as to The Priory's scale, or capacity, is the fact that there were 800 present at the ball. Before Marshall placed The Priory on the market in October 1828, it is known that he entertained the Duke of Wellington at the house in August of that year. Their connection appears to have been that Marshall had served with the Duke in the Peninsular War, in Spain.

The Priory, London Road (continued). There are few clues to The Priory's architect; however, the most likely candidate would appear to be George Allen Underwood, who was working in Cheltenham during the 1820s. Underwood was a pupil of Sir John Soane, and particularly inside The Priory there were features of possible Soanean derivation. Bryan Little instructively compared the eastern, narrow elevation of The Priory to Promenade (formerly Sundon) House, Bristol, of *c.* 1836–8 (inset). The latter might have been designed by Underwood's brother, the Bristol neo-classical architect Charles Underwood (*c.* 1791–1883).

The Priory was an accomplished Greek Revival design, crisply realised in dressed stone over a brick shell. The most arresting aspect was the powerful full-height bow on Priory Street with its giant Corinthian pilasters and their richly carved, deeply undercut capitals. The use of the Corinthian order successfully contrasted with the Greek Doric order employed within the London Road porches, with their columns *in antis*. The Priory's garden elevations were not so tidy, however, with a riot of windows and drab cement render.

A Doric porch led into the 'handsome vestibule'. The internal *tour de force* was the second-floor landing with its large circular skylight casting an ambient glow and shadows deep into the building. During the late nineteenth century The Priory passed from private domestic to institutional use, as a hostel for students at St Paul's Training College. In 1942 a letter written by an employee of the recently formed National Buildings Record mentioned in passing: 'I believe the room in which Wellington is supposed to have slept has rather a good ceiling.' However, by December 1967 demolition was planned 'during the next eight weeks', and so it was replaced with an unsightly computer centre and associated offices for Mercian Builders Ltd of Leamington Spa in 1968.

Stonycroft, St James' Square. In Bath and
North-East Somerset Library is a plan, signed
by the Bath architect Charles Harcourt
Masters (1759–?), for St James' Square,
Cheltenham, which, though never completed,
was much more ambitious than the same
architect's Royal Crescent, Cheltenham, and as
such was possibly the largest projected square
ever to grace the town. Masters' plan is not
dated, but it would be reasonable to assume a
dating of about 1808–9, when taking into
consideration associated deeds, maps and a
contemporaneous newspaper advertisement.
Recent research has shown that the north and
east coach roads were laid out more or less to
plan and, in some aspects, very accurately,
and that three houses were possibly built to
Masters' plans out of a projected sixty-five,
these being 1 St James' Square, still extant,
and a semi-detached property called
Stonycroft, the subject of this entry. Stonycroft
was positioned six plots down from no. 1, on
the north side of St James' Square.

The first-floor window surrounds of 1 St James' Square and Stonycroft can be compared with equivalents on the façade of Masters' Holburne Museum, Bath, of 1796, and it can also be said that the scale and detailing of the Square's architecture is more typical of Georgian Bath than Regency Cheltenham. Masters' St James' Square, despite its intended grandeur, was always a doomed speculation, as it took nearly twenty-five years just to lay out the north and east coach roads and to build only three houses. Stonycroft is likely to have been built between about 1820 and 1825, and possibly after Masters' death.

Fortunately various photographs were taken of Stonycroft, such as one of an entrance by the Cheltenham Civic Society, who commented in 1931: 'Note the fanlight set in lead'. This was the west end porch just discernible in George Rowe's 1836 lithograph of Jessop's Gardens (see page 14). Stonycroft had a plain and yet highly elegant interior, which had one of the finest cantilevered staircases in Cheltenham. The stairwells were oval in plan and lit by exquisite skylights that cast an ambient glow deep into the building.

By the late nineteenth century St James' Square was fast losing any private residential charm, as was indicated by Stonycroft becoming the GWR stationmaster's house, according to the 1891–2 *Cheltenham & District Post Office Directory*. It was demolished sometime after 1954.

Cambray House, Cambray Place. Cambray House was built in about 1805 on land acquired by Baynham Jones, proprietor of a nearby chalybeate spa. Also known as Wellington House, as the Duke of Wellington once stayed there, it became the first home of the Cheltenham Ladies' College. It was possibly designed by a 'Chas Wilmot Architect &c. Cheltenham', as he signed an early nineteenth-century architectural elevation depicting Cambray House and the surrounding area. Cambray House was the focal point of Cambray Place and terminated a long vista stretching from the High Street, through Cambray Place, and down to the house, which formed a neat cul-de-sac. The house was featured in S.Y. Griffith's *New Historical Description of Cheltenham* (1826). Above the ground-floor tripartite windows, on either side of the porch, was an architectural moulding unique to Cambray Place, this being a segmental scallop radiating from a sea shell. Two other houses still extant in Cambray Place have these mouldings, which would suggest that all three buildings were built at the same time and by the same architect/builder. A Victorian sale particular for Cambray House lists a cottage or lodge, double coach-house, four stall stables with a yard, and pleasure grounds stretching to the River Chelt. The house was described as a mansion containing three parlours, capital dining room and ten bedrooms. Views of the interior are extremely rare; however, there is a 1931 photograph of the vestibule door, with an exquisite internal fanlight.

Cambray's demolition in 1937, like that of Suffolk House in 1935, was an ominous and early indicator of worse to come. Suffolk and Cambray were both large, distinguished, free-standing Regency houses, situated in eye-catching locations and surrounded by large gardens clearly irresistible to the property speculator of the 1930s. Unfortunately the loss of Cambray House has damaged the integrity of an otherwise intact early Cheltenham development.

Church Street building. Formerly in Church Lane, this building was one of several which paved the way to St Mary's parish church. Church Lane was originally a footpath to the east of the church. An early reference to the lane can be found in 1736, but the building above must have been built before or during 1820, as it is on the town map of that year, or perhaps it relates to a building certificate for 'no. 1' Church Street, which was issued to Baynham Jones (of Cambray House) in 1832. It is likely to have been demolished at the same time as the Market House, then the Municipal/Public Office (and latterly the site of Tesco), which went in 1969. Note the quality of the cast-ironwork balcony. The churchyard pier in the photograph still survives to this day. The building's narrow front elevation was an especially imaginative response to an otherwise awkward site.

North Parade House, 57 Winchcombe Street. This house was probably built in the 1820s. In 1846 it became the Cheltenham Female Refuge and Home, and in 1869 a Miss Onion was matron. Architecturally it was an unusual building for Cheltenham, with its deep – almost American Deep South – veranda, which was topped by a delightful, diamond-shaped, ironwork balcony of considerable width. The balcony was supported by a series of incised square columns, in the manner of Sir John Soane. These features might suggest the hand of William Jay, an English architect who had worked in Charleston and Savannah, USA, between 1817 and 1822. Sadly North Parade House's tacky replacement is of the utmost banality.

Unidentified building. It has been suggested that the above building was situated in Winchcombe Street. A two-bay deep wrought-iron side porch, such as the one here, is an unusual arrangement for a Cheltenham building. The ironwork screen, raised on a stone base, is especially ornate. The house appears to date from the 1820s, and had clearly seen better days by the time of this photograph.

Warwick Buildings was the collective name for thirteen houses situated within a deep court off the west side of Winchcombe Street, just south of the junction with the present inner ring road. They appear to have come into existence in the 1830s and were listed in a street directory by 1841. In 1935 Warwick Buildings was earmarked for demolition in slum clearance programme number two. Dr Steven Blake has written that the houses were 'once an attractive cul-de-sac, enclosed by railings and with iron bollards preventing vehicular access; the tall house at the western end has a fine ironwork porch'.

House in Warwick Place. Warwick Place was in existence by at least 1830, when nos 8–10 were listed in the 1830 *Directory*. The above photograph, taken in 1972, shows two properties; the bow on the right belongs to a separate building. By 1976 Warwick Place was derelict and beyond repair, and the local press could report 'the block of decaying properties which local traders complain of so bitterly'. To the left of the above property was a yard, which by 1976 was used as 'one huge rubbish dump'. Clearly Warwick Place had seen better days. The site is now occupied by the Friends Meeting House.

Farnley Lodge (YMCA), Vittoria Walk. Farnley Lodge was built sometime between 1820 and 1826. The porch's four Ionic columns, mirrored by rear pilasters, appear to be based on the Temple of Ilissus – a classical order ubiquitously employed in Cheltenham at this period. David Verey described the porch in 1970 as 'a pleasant detached tetrastyle Ionic portico'. In 1931 Farnley was a Cheltenham Ladies' College boarding house and by 1970 a YMCA. The porch has since gone but the rest of the building flourishes to this day as the town's YMCA.

The Rock House, Vittoria Walk. Possibly Cheltenham's most idiosyncratic building of all time, The Rock House can trace its origins back to 1815, when it was known as Waterloo Cottage. However, in 1842 Waterloo Cottage was either demolished or massively remodelled, and it was renamed Rockville, and later still The Rock House.

Who built or designed The Rock House? According to Michael Lyon, a former resident between about 1940 and 1950, 'All the work was said to have been done by Italian craftsmen'. More realistically, however, it was perhaps the work of one T. Newman, a grotto builder, who resided at Swiss Cottage, Bayshill, according to the 1844 town directory.

The façade was clad in a chocolate-coloured rock, speckled with a contrasting lighter-coloured rock, and conches – all rather like the internal lining of a grotto turned inside out. A prominent white, wooden, dentilled cornice made an unusual contrast to the rich cladding. The roof had fish scale tiles and four prominent chimney-stacks covered in the same cladding. The first-floor bedroom windows of the main block were attractively glazed with small multiple panes, and had distinctive relieving arches, picked out in the lighter-coloured rock.

If the exterior was extraordinary, then the interior was quite simply bizarre. There are at least two known photographs of the 'conservatory', later to become the hall. This room was a grotto with asymmetrical openings and arches, supposedly constructed from the ballast of Captain Hardy's ship. Like the exterior, there were conches and fossils set into the ballast. Even the window glazing bars were constructed of the ballast. Lyon recalls: 'The most extraordinary part was the hall which was a Rock Grotto. The rock looked very very solid and curved up from a heavily stone slabbed floor to a domed roof. Inserted and apparently growing out of this curved rock face were many different types and colours of coral, fossilised turtles, fossil jellyfish, etc., and from the roof growing down were stalactites, some of watery yellow appearance. Three deeply recessed tunnels ended in glass panes and small views of the greenhouse.' Sadly this unashamedly eccentric building was demolished in spring 1978, and in 1979 six nondescript maisonettes were built on the site.

Wolseley House, Vittoria Walk. Wolseley House began life as Lindsay Cottage, named after Lady Mary Lindsay who stayed there, and was built in about 1805. In 1809 the then owner, Captain George Brisac RN, late of HMS *Iris*, was in the dock for erecting poles and rattles outside the Cottage. The 1812 Cheltenham guidebook noted 'Lady Mary Lindsay's singular but elegant "Cottage"' – a Regency euphemism for a large house. Some time after 1820 it was enlarged as Wolseley Villa, and later still was known as Wolseley House. Wolseley House sat in large grounds, which stretched from Oriel Road to almost halfway up Vittoria Walk. The house was a substantial yet plain, stucco affair. It had two main external features, a porch with paired Tuscan columns and a two-storey bow on the garden front. In 1853 Wolseley was advertised for sale, and was described as having a 'spacious Entrance Hall, Dining Room, Drawing Room, Ante Room, Library, Four best Bed Rooms, Two Dressing Rooms, Water Closets, Three Servants' Bed Rooms' and 'luxuriant Shrubberies and Lawns tastefully laid out'.

By the early twentieth century Wolseley had become 'Soyer's Hotel, En Pension'; it was advertised in the 1908 town directory as being 'High-class only' and as having 'Ices always ready'. Accompanying the advertisement are two rare photographs of the house surrounded by lawn, trees, shrubs and paths. The scene is quite halcyon, with people playing croquet on a lawn – one which would eventually become tarmac. The front elevation of Wolseley was five bays wide, with a recessed centre, and there was much use of quoins and rustication at ground-floor level. Later encroached upon by various unsightly outbuildings, when it became a telephone exchange in 1933, Wolseley was eventually demolished, perhaps in the 1960s, in order to make way for the even more unsightly exchange there today.

The Great House was erected in 1730 on the site of Cheltenham's original Manor House. The above drawing, now in the V&A, London, is by the distinguished eighteenth-century Rococo artist Thomas Robins. The Great House stood in landscaped grounds entered by a sweeping drive with impressive pillared gates, on the site of the former Barnby Bendall storage warehouse in St George's Place. The Great House, also known as Grove House, later became Mrs Field's boarding-house and as such was the 'centre of Cheltenham's social life for over 100 years'. In 1780 it was described thus: 'a large stately

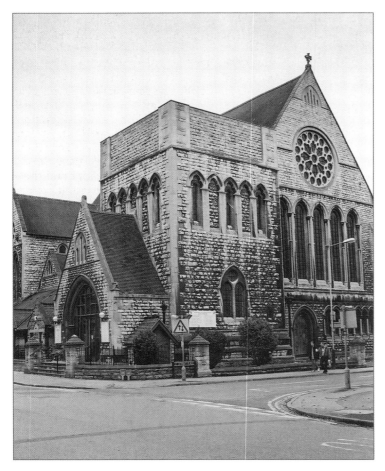

mansion of modern structure . . . the chief part of which is generally let out in commodious lodgings for the company'. The Great House's simple early Georgian architecture was L-shaped in plan, with a block to the west – presumably for lodging. The main block was of five bays, three storeys and fenestrated with emphatic voussoirs above the windows. The rear elevation had the ubiquitous central, canted bow found throughout eighteenth-century domestic architecture. This handsome house – not unworthy of an architect such as Francis Smith of Warwick, who worked at nearby Sandywell Park – was demolished in 1859 and replaced by Ewan Christian's St Matthew's (1877–9).

Gothic Cottage, Portland Street. A highly unusual Gothic façade for Cheltenham, possibly of five bays and definitely of two storeys, and perhaps dating from the 1820s. It has been described as a 'Charming little house called "Gothic"'. The central bay was defined by two full height 'classical' pilasters from which sprang an ogival arch over the first-floor window. All the windows had ogival, almost 'Moorish' arches, and there was unusual lozenge-shaped window glazing. In 1847 the house was referred to as 'Gothic Cottage, opposite Trinity Church'. In 1891 Gothic Cottage was home to Mrs Bridgeman and the Misses Mason, dressmakers. John Piper illustrated this building, as a detail (reproduced below), within his Cheltenham panorama for John Betjeman's *First and Last Loves* (1952). Piper captioned it '"Gothic", Portland Street'. Projecting forward of this building was a more conventional Regency house of three storeys and three bays, with bracketed eaves. This house had a fine porch, with entablature and a deep dentil course, approached by steps. The site is now a municipal car park. The photograph above dates from 1966.

Portland Tabernacle. The Portland Tabernacle was originally known as Seymour Hall, or 13 Portland Street. By 1891 it was known as Handel Hall, having undergone a conversion for the purposes of worship in the late nineteenth century. In 1898 it became the Portland Tabernacle and during the twentieth century was known as the Portland Street Church of Christ. Seymour Hall was built as a private residence by 1818 for Robert Hughes, scion of a prominent Cheltenham family since 1749. Robert Hughes was a Whig, an attorney and a local landowner, responsible for founding the Cheltenham Masonic lodge in 1818.

Seymour Hall was an exemplary example of Sir John Soane's influence in the provinces, the façade being an astylar elevation of Soanean derivation. Such a design could well be the work of George Allen Underwood, the prolific Cheltenham architect of the Regency period. The most conclusive indicator of a pupil of Soane's hand is to be found in the design of the delicate balcony. This is a virtual facsimile of the first-floor balcony at 12 and 14 Lincoln's Inn Fields, London, designed by Soane in 1792 and 1824. Seymour Hall was advertised in 1827, just after Hughes's death in that year, by the *Cheltenham Journal* thus: 'A Very substantial Stone-built DWELLING-HOUSE, being No. 13, Portland Street. . . . The whole of the elegant and genuine London furniture, made purposely for the house by *Wilkinson*, *Norris*, and *Collins*, may be taken to at the option of the purchaser.' The fact that the furniture was made to order for the building indicates some serious pretensions to grandeur.

The Portland Tabernacle was demolished in about 1979–80 in order to make way for Cheltenham's Northern Relief Road, and the property's deeds were deposited with the Gloucestershire Record Office in 1979. In the words of David Verey, it was 'a charming but ungrammatical neo-Greek panelled stone façade of three storeys and three bays, the upper windows round-headed. Good wrought-iron balcony on the first floor.' The much-maligned Millennium Restaurant was built more or less on the site in the late 1990s, and has been empty virtually ever since.

The Elms, Swindon Road. The Elms is one of several important private residences featured in S.Y. Griffith's *New Historical Description of Cheltenham* (1826) to have been demolished. It is now hard to believe that The Elms was once situated near the now decaying, polluted and noisy Swindon Road; however, judging from Griffith's 1826 view it must have been a most pleasant area. The Elms first appears on the 1820 town map and was built for Sir Robert Ricketts. The elevation facing the Swindon Road was eight bays long, with a central pediment and a bowed wing to one side. The house sat in large grounds with a tree-lined avenue: the above view is from the garden side. In 1883 The Elms, by now a Workhouse of the Guardians of the Poor Union, was massively extended by J.T. Darby, architect of the Winter Garden, to include an extra storey. During the Second World War the building was used by the army. It was eventually demolished in November 1979 and replaced with low-rise housing of little imagination. All that remains now are the brick boundary walls, the stumps of the stone gate piers on the Swindon Road (in front of Pope's Close, which was built in the grounds of The Elms), and a tall Victorian gate pier on the far left of the property, next to the entrance (opposite). It is built of red and dark brick, stone trimmings and has a stone pedimented cap. A solitary gate hook remains.

Field Lodge. According to J.K. Griffith's *Cheltenham Guide* (1818) a spa once on this site, and now situated in Sandford Park, was discovered in 1802. Of the Original Chalybeate Spa, Griffith noted:

This spring had been observed for many years to issue out of the side of a bank in a very sparing quantity, depositing in its course a yellow ochery matter. The common people drank it successfully as a lotion in weaknesses, and other complaints of the eyes. It was not, however, till the beginning of 1802, that it attracted particular attention, when it was found to be a small branch of a very copious spring, originating in a meadow within a few hundred paces. Upon sinking a well in a proper situation, it was found to produce equal to any demand. Mr. Barrett, the proprietor, has built a commodious room for the company, and also laid out gravelled walks to the upper part of the town, from which it is distant but a few hundred yards.

By 1834 the Original Chalybeate Spa had become Chalybeate Spa Villa, and by the time of the first OS map of Cheltenham, surveyed in 1884, the site had become Field Lodge and was a private dwelling. Between 1886 and 1927 it was the home of the James family, Edward James being evicted by the Council in 1927. The façade of this building survives, albeit in a heavily mutilated condition, as an electrical substation in the corner of Sandford Park.

Cranley, Wellington Square. Cranley (also known as Cranley Lodge) was originally known as The Aviary, and is one of the few early nineteenth-century houses to have been demolished at Pittville. It might just have been the work of William Jay, for in January 1826 the *Gloucester Herald* reported, regarding the burgeoning Pittville estate, that 'some very elegant houses are completing on various spots under the superintendence of Mr. William Jay, a gentleman whose architectural merits are most admirably displayed in every task he has hitherto undertaken'. Unfortunately the *Herald* is not specific about which houses Jay built, but perhaps he was involved with the four on the north side of Wellington Square that belong to the earliest phase of the estate's development, which date from 1826–9 and perhaps bear some of Jay's hallmarks. Cranley was enlarged in 1897 with a west-facing extension and an additional storey, all carried out in a most incongruous mock-Tudor idiom. The house was demolished in 1986 and replaced with the present flats.

Selkirk Villa, Pittville Circus.
Selkirk Villa was built before 1817. In
1817 it was the home of the dissenting
minister Mr Snow, and for a while was
briefly licensed as a place of worship.
In 1819 the *Cheltenham Chronicle*
advertised Selkirk Villa for let, listing:
'a handsome Dining-Room and
Drawing-Room, with a very extensive
prospect; a good third Sitting-Room;
five excellent Bed-Rooms', and so on.
The house was mentioned in passing
in an 1820 guidebook to Cheltenham:
'The road is enlivened by Selkirk Villa,
Oaklands, &c.' In 1948 Paul Reilly
included a plate of Selkirk Villa in his
Introduction to Regency Architecture and
captioned it: 'A balconied bay in
Pittville Circus, Cheltenham (*c.* 1825)'.
Note the unusual curvature –
especially as it approaches the wall – of
the veranda 'tenting' seen here,
photographed in 1968. Later
subsumed into Pittville Circus as
Tresmere, it was eventually demolished
in the 1970s.

Radley Gazebo, Scoriton/Fern Lawn, Pittville Crescent. Scoriton, once known as Fern Lawn, is a substantial, undistinguished Victorian house on the edge of the salubrious Pittville estate, Cheltenham. It was probably built in the 1860s as a typical, prosperous middle-class home. Its redeeming feature was the large garden, occupying between a quarter and a third of the crescent where Scoriton is situated. Sale particulars from 1909 present the house and grounds at a luxuriant peak during that Edwardian Indian Summer, not long before the First World War. However, as early as 1909 the property was offered as potentially ripe for splitting into several properties, including 'a charming and matured site for the erection of a Gentleman's Residence'. Nevertheless the grounds somehow survived intact until the 1950s, when the house itself was subdivided into flats and the owners moved into a purpose-built bungalow, named Radley, in the grounds. This, too, has now been demolished.

In the 1980s a further property was squeezed into a plot between the 1950s bungalow and Scoriton itself. The twentieth century's impact on Scoriton's fortunes – a tale of subdivision and asset-stripping – serves as a reflective microcosm of Cheltenham's architectural and landscape plight, and perhaps the built heritage at large.

In the corner of the bungalow's garden was a Victorian gazebo roughly contemporaneous with Scoriton. Little is known of the gazebo's history, and in particular when it was built, but by examining historic town maps one can narrow down its erection to between 1864 and 1884. The gazebo (pictured opposite, top, in 1986) was a substantial wooden structure of nine sides, over an underground cavity, and was painted in two tones of light blue, with windows on five sides. The only known reference to the gazebo is from the 1909 sale particular description: 'one ornamental octagonal and two rustic Summer Houses'. The two rustic summerhouses have long since disappeared, as has the gazebo, which was sold at auction in April 1999 for £800.

Marle Hill, Evesham Road. Marle Hill was another of the early Regency houses to grace the town, but before the nearby Pittville estate was developed in the 1820s it was isolated and in the countryside. The earliest reference to it is from 1806, when Thomas Delabere sold a part of the 72 acre New Barn Farm (Rosehill) to Francis Welles of Marle Hill, the likely builder of the house in the early 1810s. The earliest view, above, of the house belongs to the 1820 guidebook to Cheltenham, which contains a written description: 'The road is enlivened by Selkirk Villa, Oaklands, &c.; and at a distance of about half a mile to the left, is discovered a charming mansion, called Marl [*sic*] Hill, the residence of R. Capper, esq. It is situated on an eminence, surrounded with delightful pleasure-grounds, designed by taste, and executed by the hand of judgement. The lodge, leading to the seat, adjoins the New Evesham road, and is about half a mile from Cheltenham.'

Marle Hill was an extremely simple Regency house of five bays and three storeys, the only feature being, before the addition of a somewhat fussy Victorian 'carriage porch of open arches in stone work', a central bow. The house was built principally of ashlar-dressed stone and contained five reception rooms.

The grounds were extensive with three entrance lodges and a boathouse on the lake – all of which have gone, except for a single Victorian lodge on Marle Hill Road. Marle Hill was Cheltenham's only example of a private landscape park, which survives largely intact as a public park and boating lake. The estate was purchased by Cheltenham Borough Council in 1931 for £6,500, and the house was demolished in the 1960s or 1970s, to be replaced with a nondescript housing estate.

Alstone Lawn, Gloucester Road. Alstone Lawn was a large double-bowed house, built before 1820 in what was then outside Cheltenham, but by the time of its demolition in about 1933 it had become integrated into the suburbs. It is marked on the 1820 Post Office map as the residence of W.H. Prescod Esq. In the Cheltenham Museum collection is a charming lithograph by Henry Lamb of the house, perhaps the only known view. The house was a classic Regency composition of two full-height bows, stucco façade, three storeys, with balancing wings of one storey and two bays wide. Architecturally it had much in common with Suffolk House, Suffolk Square (see page 156). The wings were very high in comparison to the scale of the main block. Each wing had two large windows on either side of a central niche. The house was approached by a circular carriage sweep passing through the grounds, and surrounded by a variety of trees and shrubs; there were also a couple of garden seats – one in the fashionable rustic style. Of particular interest is a summerhouse, partly hidden in the background foliage, on the far right. It appears to have been in the rustic style, circular and with stilts supporting a tapered roof. The 1888 OS map is topographically informative and makes a worthwhile comparison with Lamb's 1810 view. It shows the house approached by a long drive, which had a lodge on the Gloucester Road. The grounds had various outbuildings and orchards. All this was cleared for council housing in the early 1930s.

Alstone Lodge, Gloucester Road. Alstone Lodge was neighbour to Alstone Lawn, both once on the Gloucester Road. It was situated behind the Victorian terrace pictured below. Alstone Lodge was advertised in the *Cheltenham Chronicle* in June 1810 as 'newly erected'. Fortunately the house is recorded in attractive sale particulars dating from 1881 and 8 May 1894. For a house built in 1810 it appears rather Victorian, which might therefore suggest that Alstone was remodelled, perhaps in the 1840s or 1850s, in a fashionable Italianate style. Alstone Lodge and its garden were probably built over at a similar time to Alstone Lawn, in about 1933.

Grovefield Villa, Gloucester Road. Grovefield Villa was once situated almost hard on the Gloucester Road and opposite the woodland of Arle Court. On stylistic grounds Grovefield has been dated to about the first decade of the nineteenth century. In 1834 the property was purchased by Thomas Butt, who later commissioned, in 1858, the 'more seriously Tudor' Arle Court. In 1885 Grovefield was advertised for sale as 'containing Four Bed Rooms; on the Ground Floor – Two Sitting Rooms, Kitchen . . . together with a large Garden; the frontage to turnpike road is 184 feet'. Grovefield Villa was demolished in about 1967, the year of the above photograph, in order to make way for the County Council's widening of the Gloucester Road.

Ashfield, Bayshill Road. If Ashfield was originally known as 'Italian Villa Bay's Hill' (1845), then it was built between 1840 and 1845, but if always known as Ashfield it was built in 1860. Ashfield was a two-storey building in a sub-Italianate manner. It had attractive arched windows on both floors and ponderous balconies on scrolled brackets. In 1896 Ashfield was put on the market as a 'Detached Freehold Residence, beautifully situated on high ground. . . . The Residence is approached by a carriage sweep, and contains three spacious and lofty Reception Rooms, viz., elegant double Drawing Room and well-proportioned Dining Room. . . . The Surrounding Grounds are over half an acre in extent, and are tastefully laid out in well-turfed lawns . . . and [with] a Summer House.' The view opposite was taken in April 1971; the house was demolished in 1989. Its replacement, Ashfield House, above, was built in 1999 by Crosby Homes. In 1983 Gavin Stamp complained about the 'illiteracy' of Postmodernism, and in the replacement of Ashfield we have a good example, with pilasters and a classical order surely worthy of a Disney set.

No. 4 Fauconberg Villas, Bayshill Road. Fauconberg Villas was formerly a terrace of four free-standing villas designed by Samuel Onley, architect of the demolished Winchcombe Street Congregational chapel and various other Cheltenham buildings. In July 1861 the *Cheltenham Looker-On* noted: 'Fauconberg Villas, recently built by Mr. Onley'. Nos 1 and 2 were first listed in the 1862 *Cheltenham Directory* and no. 3 was listed by 1867. This would suggest therefore that no. 4 was built in about 1867. In 1941 Sir Hugh Casson wrote: 'Fauconberg Villas are not and do not pretend to be examples of great architecture. They are just simple, stuccoed town-houses, with the pleasant proportions and restrained ornament of their period, and so unassuming in appearance that the casual passer-by would perhaps never even notice them. In this unobtrusiveness, however, lies much of their charm. They were designed not as isolated buildings, but as part of a street – units of a composition in which the other houses, trees, railings and the curving slope of the road itself also play their parts. They fulfil this function with such admirable dignity and good manners that it is to be hoped that no scheme of "improvement" will ever condemn them to mutilation or neglect.' No. 4 was demolished in 1968 in order to make way for a new entrance to Cheltenham Ladies' College on Bayshill Road. The picture opposite is taken from a view by Stanley J. Dent and dates from 1948.

Bays Hill Lodge, Parabola Road. Bays Hill Lodge was built in 1780 or 1781, perhaps by William Skillicorne, for Lord Fauconberg. The Bays Hill name is first noted in 1605 as 'Beues hill', or 'Bayes hill'. Bays Hill Lodge must have been the most important dwelling to have been built in Cheltenham since the 1730 Great House. In 1786 the Lodge was described thus: 'A house lately built . . . on an eminence, commands a most extensive and beautiful prospect.' It was built from bricks dug out of the clay on the site. George III stayed here on his seminal visit to the developing spa town in 1788. Their Majesties were accompanied by the Princess Royal, Princess Augusta and Princess Elizabeth from 12 July to 16 August 1788. Originally known as Fauconberg House, it had become Bays Hill Lodge by 1800. Considered 'an old-fashioned brick building' by 1845, it was demolished in 1855 and replaced by Sussex Lodge in Parabola Road. In November 1855 it was 'about to be pulled down . . . in order to make way for a modern villa, to be erected on its beautiful site by Mr. Darby'. Bays Hill Lodge had been quite a large establishment, with a square-plan stable courtyard behind the mansion block – the former backed on to a Lads Lane. Unusually narrow for its height, the sub-Palladian Bays Hill Lodge was somewhat ungainly in terms of design.

Fauconberg Terrace was first listed in the 1866 directory for Cheltenham, which might suggest that it was built in that year. The best description of the terrace is to be found in Cecily Steadman's *In the Days of Miss Beale* (1930): 'Fauconberg Terrace is disproportionately high and narrow for its length and when first built was unofficially known after its builder as "Onley's Folly". When the Ladies' College bought it, it was said to be unsafe, and much work had to be done to put it into order. Even then, it oscillated violently in a high wind. There were eighty-six stairs from the basement to the top storey, and though in our house there was a service lift it was so small and worked so jerkily that it could only be used for coal scuttles. The maids' work, therefore, had to be very carefully planned to avoid overdoing them.' This rather unloved terrace of six properties, designed by Samuel Onley, was demolished only four years after Steadman's account, in 1934, and replaced with the neo-Cotswold West Wing of the Ladies' College in 1936.

Nos 4 and 5 Bayshill Lawn, Parabola Road. Bayshill Lawn originally referred to a series of five houses on the north side of Parabola Road. They were mostly completed by 1840. Nos 4 and 5, also known as Bayshill Lawn, were a pair of substantial semi-detached late Regency houses, with stucco elevations of considerable gravitas. Architecturally they take their cue from the series of large Greek Revival houses on Bayshill Road. In 1883 no. 5 was purchased by Cheltenham Ladies' College for £2,357 for use as a boarding house. The adjacent house, no. 4, was purchased in 1903 and the two were combined into one. In the early twentieth century two postcards, featuring different vantage points, were published of the building – valuable documentation of an otherwise obscure building. Bayshill Lawn was bombed on 11 December 1940, subsequently demolished and replaced – albeit not until 1960 – by the present Elizabeth House.

Boltons, Christchurch Road. Christchurch Road – not that it was called this – first appears on the 1840 map of Cheltenham. Boltons, probably a twentieth-century name, is near impossible to date as we do not know its original name, which would have enabled a date of erection to be determined by consulting the year-by-year directories of the Victorian period. However, it was clearly a Victorian house of substantial proportions. The double-storey bow, or bombé, is unusually pronounced for a Victorian building; a canted bay is more usually associated with Victorian domestic architecture. The house was demolished in 1974.

Abbeyholme, Overton Road, was always something of an architectural interloper, even within Cheltenham's comparatively small stock of Gothic Revival housing. Originally known as Westholme, Abbeyholme was designed in 1866 by the architect John Middleton as his own home. The family moved in in 1868 and sold up in 1884. Legend has it that Middleton spent about £80,000 on building the house, importing Continental craftsmen, as well as the best of those in the Cotswolds, to execute the beautiful stone- and plasterwork and panelling. The tiles around the fireplaces were reputedly by William Morris and Sir Edward Burne-Jones.

David Verey described Abbeyholme as being 'in [the] French-Gothic style, an innovation for domestic building in Cheltenham', and of the exterior he noted: 'Of rock-faced rusticated stone with freestone dressings, a steep-pitched tile roof and tower, and a small oriel window projecting to a point'. Elsewhere, Abbeyholme has been described 'a major example of . . . Pre-Raphaelite type architecture'. Parts of the building were salvaged by the Bowes Museum, County Durham, and Cheltenham Art Gallery and Museum. Abbeyholme's demolition in 1973 was covered by the local press: 'The rescued panelling is said to be Oregon pine, a rich browny-red, with painted transfer paper work in greens and creams and gold, which still retain their original lustre after 100 years. The museum [Bowes] is also taking away doors, and hope to persuade the demolishers to extract a carved window as well. This window is on ecclesiastical lines, with intricate and meticulous carving up the sides, stone angels just above eye-level and Gothic ornamentation round the glazing.' The article continued: 'There has been a sort of national scandal among preservation bodies and the Victorian Society, and they were concerned about the demolition of this major piece of domestic architecture.'

Internally there were sumptuously carved fireplaces, intricate brass door handle plates and deeply undercut corbel sculptures supporting pillars of fine marbles or stones, such as granite or Purbeck. One corbel was so deeply undercut with angels and flowers that it was almost a free-standing sculpture. Because of this approach Abbeyholme represented a near perfect Pre-Raphaelite synthesis of architecture, painting and sculpture. The house originally stood in grounds of 1 acre.

Nos 1 and 2 Lansdown Crescent. In 1824–5 Pearson Thompson laid out the Lansdown Estate on lands purchased by his father, Henry Thompson, in 1801. By 1829 twenty houses had been built on the estate. Pearson's chosen architect was J.B. Papworth, who proposed a 'Circular Plot' and 'Streight [*sic*] Plot' in 1825. The 'Circular Plot' proposed villas, as opposed to a terrace. However, Papworth had built only nos 1 and 2 by 1829; this was before the Jearrads gained control of the estate in 1829–30. From 1831 the rest (no. 3 onwards) of the huge convex crescent was built to a different design by the Jearrads. No. 1 was unusual in that it was the only Papworth house in Cheltenham to be faced in stone and not stucco. David Verey considered no. 1's pedimented windows, and porch with columns *in antis*, to be 'more refined than those on the rest of the crescent.' No. 1 was demolished in 1968 and replaced in facsimile in 1985.

Netherleigh, Lansdown Road. Netherleigh was built in 1874 or 1875 and its first resident was a J. Brown. The photograph opposite was taken in about 1905. Netherleigh, judging from the photograph, was a very solid and substantial house of three storeys, with a typically Victorian canted ground-floor bay window. Ornamentation was confined to the slightly unusual cornice within the eaves and to the areas of fenestration. The date of Netherleigh's demolition is not known; however, the blocks of flats now on the site appear to date from the 1970s.

Cambray Pavilion, Bath Road. Cambray Pavilion, once known as Cambray Villa, was built before 1806 for James King, Master of the Ceremonies in the summer season at Cheltenham. It was described in 1806 as being 'a villa, which in point of taste and elegance may vie with any modern building whatever'. Despite its current appearance this part of town, developed after 1802, had once been a fashionable area, as is suggested by an 1809 diarist: 'the Bath Road, plots of this land are selling on Building Leases for immense prices'. Architecturally it was somewhat unorthodox. Perhaps this is best explained by the strange proportions: overall rather squat; an overly dominant portico; and the unusual deployment of segmental windows at first-floor level. Maps indicate that the rear elevation was double-bowed and facing the River Chelt and Cambray Meadow, an area which would eventually become the

present Sandford Park in 1928. Cambray Pavilion sat in a large garden, which eased down to the Chelt. This fine Regency villa, which had 'Ten lofty and airy Bed Rooms', was demolished in 1929 and replaced with a garage. The site is now occupied by the Moon under Water drinking house.

The Wellington Mansion, Bath Road and Wellington Street. Originally known as Cambray House, the Wellington Mansion was yet another early, though short-lived, Cheltenham residence. It was built in about 1807 for Colonel John Riddell, a retired army officer. The Wellington Mansion was let to the Duke of Wellington on several occasions and therefore acquired his distinguished name in 1816. Wellington also stayed at The Priory and Cambray House in Cambray Place – both now demolished. The only known views of the Wellington Mansion are from the garden, facing the River Chelt. The front of the house probably faced Bath Street, as the carriage drive was on this side. The Wellington Mansion, having been pulled down and its materials sold at auction in September 1843, was converted in 1862 into a nursery garden. All that remains of this important house is, as is so often the case, a solitary stone boundary pier on the Bath Road, next to the River Chelt.

This highly eroded pier is actually one of the piers – once belonging to a bridge – depicted in a view (above) of the house and grounds in S.Y. Griffith's *New Historical Description of Cheltenham* (1826).

Mosquito Ghur, 143 Bath Road. With Malcolm Ghur, now Pillar House and further along the Bath Road, Mosquito Ghur must lay claim to the title of 'most exotic house name ever' within Cheltenham. Mosquito Ghur probably alludes to an Anglo-Indian connection of the 'Curry and Colonels' cliché, 'Ghur' being Hindi for house. The house was in existence as Mosquito Ghur by 1828, when it was advertised for auction in the *Cheltenham Journal*. In 1877 a Mr Chick lived here. For a humble, two-storey, artisan house, Mosquito Ghur had disproportionately complex ironwork – so much so that it was featured in Paul Reilly's *Introduction to Regency Architecture* (1948), where it is described as 'rich ironwork in Bath Road, Cheltenham'. The Cheltenham Civic Society, who took the photograph on the left, noted in 1931 that 'even small houses had nice ironwork'. This photograph conveys the arid, overgrown, sleepy, perhaps even colonial feel of the place, which was lost for ever with the savage removal of the fine ironwork veranda and the perhaps appropriate, or at least coincidental, erection of what is now the Balti Walla restaurant over the front garden.

Sandford Place/Bath Road. This wing or link between two buildings, once part of Nazareth House, was situated in Sandford Place, Bath Road, opposite Cheltenham College. Sandford Place was in existence by 1819 but it is not known when the above section was built. Nazareth House, a Roman Catholic home for old people and orphans, was demolished in 1969. It was on the site of the present Century Court development.

Newick House, 101 Bath Road. Newick House was an austere Regency dwelling of four bays and three storeys, with an ashlar façade and brick side elevations. It had ground-floor French windows with shutters terminated by unmoulded semi-circular heads – recessed into the elevation. There were deep roof eaves and a low single-storey wing to the right. The house is possibly on Bettison's *c*. 1819 map of Cheltenham; it was certainly in existence by 1837, when it was listed in the *Cheltenham Annuaire* for that year. Newick was taken over by Mr Watson-Smyth in the 1840s as a part of Cheltenham College, and in time it was to become the College's oldest boarding house, so perhaps the large rear extension was added at a later date in order to provide further accommodation. Later renamed Corinth House, it was demolished in the early 1980s. Newick's replacement, also known as Corinth House, was built in 1985 and is a classic example of 1980s Postmodernism by numbers.

Thirlestaine House Gate. Thirlestaine House was built for James Robert Scott (1790–1832), son of Robert Scott, minister at Innerleithen, Scotland, between 1820 and 1831, when works ground to a halt owing to the former's financial embarrassments. An incomplete Thirlestaine House was sold therefore to Lord Northwick in 1838 by Scott's younger brother, Alexander, a close friend of Lord Byron. Between 1838 and 1855 Northwick embarked on an almost non-stop campaign of picture gallery building, which resulted in ten sumptuous galleries.

Although it is known that George Allen Underwood designed the stables at Thirlestaine House, there is no trace of his often Soanean hand within the mainstream Greek Revival house itself. However, it is likely that Underwood designed the 'lofty brick walls, with noble entrance gates'. The demolished main entrance on the Bath Road, opposite, was emphatically Soanean in design. The boundary walls were known well into the last century as 'Scott's walls', and they were pulled down in August 1949. Traces, however, especially boundary piers, survive in Thirlestaine Road and Kew Place.

Thirlestaine House Stables. In 1822 *The Annals of Sporting and Fancy Gazette* published a considerable two-part article on the stables James Robert Scott was building at Thirlestaine House. Scott appears to have wasted no time in getting this outlier up and running (unlike the house), as it was fully functional by 1822. The article is useful on many accounts. It confirms, albeit circumstantially, that Thirlestaine was started in 1820, the year before Scott became a Town Commissioner, reporting: 'Horses which formerly were subject to the complaints incident to their being kept in common stables, have now been two years in this stable without one case of sickness or complaint of any kind having occurred.' The *Gazette* was particularly impressed by the humane way in which Scott kept horses in his 'little Temple of Hippona'. The neo-Georgian architect A.E. Richardson chose to illustrate the stables, with a detail of one of the two Choragic Monuments of Lysicrates that once crowned the roof, in his *The Smaller English House of the Later Renaissance, 1660–1830* (1925). The stables were converted to residential use for Cheltenham College by Louis de Soissons in about 1948.

Bath Road Entrance Lodges. Two lodges, as opposed to one, for a building the size of Thirlestaine House is perhaps surprising. A photograph of one of them, above, survives in the National Monuments Record, Swindon. It shows a single-storey, canted structure built into Thirlestaine's boundary wall. The principal elevation had three windows. The high ratio of window to wall for such a small building is explained by the fact that there would have been no windows at the back of the lodge, as this was the private boundary wall, facing the Bath Road. On either side of the entrance to the lodge were a couple of stone substitute, classical frieze roundels – a typically Lord Northwick touch; he was the owner from

1838. These lodges had been built by 1831, as they were referred to in a sale particular of that year: 'Two Lodges . . . [with] Sleeping Rooms.' The 1841 census lists the two lodges as having a couple living in each. William Court, soon to be Lord Northwick's House Steward, and his wife Eliza lived in 'Lodge No. 2'. The lodges were demolished some time after the Second World War. All that survives is a blocked-up former entrance to the Kew Place lodge (right).

Lindley, College Road. It is difficult to determine when exactly Lindley was built, but judging from maps of the town a date somewhere between 1864 and 1878 would seem plausible. Moreover, as late as 1864 there was not even a single building on College Road. Lindley was a freestanding Victorian house of a slightly unorthodox design. One of the best features was the porch, which was executed in stone as opposed to the contrasting stucco elevations. The porch had fluted Ionic columns on a raised base. Inscribed on the entablature lintel was 'music' in Greek, which is a reference to the fact that Lindley was Cheltenham College's Music School from 1915 to 1977. When compared with the rest of the building, the porch still retained an aesthetical hangover from the Regency. Lindley was demolished sometime after 1982.

All that remains are four stone boundary piers on College and Sandford Road. They have pediments and are decorated with blind arches. One on College Road is inscribed 'Lindley', indicating that it was the original entrance pier. The porch entablature and a fluted column drum survive – as a sad pile of stones – near the Accident and Emergency entrance to Cheltenham General Hospital on College Road.

Cheltondale, College Road. 'Architectural abortions' is how the *Cheltenham Looker-On* described, in July 1868, a series of newly built Cheltenham College boarding houses dating from the 1860s. Four were built by the Boarding Houses Company and Cheltondale, once on the junction of College Road and Orrisdale Terrace, was the last of the series. Cheltondale was designed by the prolific Victorian Cheltenham architect John Middleton in 1867, a building certificate was issued in 1868 and it was ready for occupation in 1869. The builders were W.C. and L. Channon. John Middleton was responsible for several Cheltenham churches, such as All Saints', St Stephen's and Holy Apostles', as well as Cheltenham Ladies' College. Architecturally Cheltondale was a large polychromatic building in a sub-William Butterfield manner and with plate tracery windows. All four were in a similar architectural style and enjoyed, for the period, superior amenities compared with the earlier non-purpose-built boarding houses. Cheltondale was demolished in about 1982.

Glasshouse, Stratford House, Suffolk Square. Glasshouses are ephemeral at the best of times, and yet there is something rather engaging about this one, formerly in Suffolk Square. Perhaps the unusually graphic depiction, as would be expected of a ready-to-order catalogue, is more interesting than the structure itself. The glasshouse has long gone and in its place is a raised, balconied area. The bank and canted canopy to the left have been completely cleared away and replaced by a sunken area, contemporaneous with the aforementioned raised section. Although Stratford House appears to date from the early 1830s (certainly pre-1834), the actual glasshouse looks to be very much a typically Victorian improvement – it is an addition to a small wing. The house itself is a late essay in Greek Revival.

Suffolk House, Suffolk Square. With the possible exception of The Casino at Painswick Lawn, Suffolk House was the first major Cheltenham house to be demolished, and in the process set a precedent for the next forty to fifty years. It is unfortunate that Suffolk House – out of all the houses in Suffolk Square – had to go, bearing in mind that it was the oldest building in the area. Suffolk House was built as early as 1804 by Joseph Rainger, a builder, at a time when Cheltenham was still in its architectural infancy. Rainger came to Cheltenham in 1804 from Wiltshire, where he had been a tenant farmer and builder on the estates of the Earls of Suffolk and Berkshire, near Malmesbury. Suffolk House can be counted among a first wave of important early buildings, which included Hygeia House, Vittoria Walk, Royal Crescent and the Liberal Club, North Place. However, the origins of Suffolk House were in fact eighteenth-century: it was built on the site of Gallipot Farm, which in turn had medieval origins, and was mentioned in the 1783 guidebook to Cheltenham thus: 'Just above the well is a farm-house, known by the name of Gallipot, to which parties are made for tea, syllabub, & c.' In 1811 Anne Rushout noted in her diary: 'Go to Cheltenham on a visit to Sir C. Cockerell [of Sezincote, Glos.] who has taken Lord Suffolk's house.'

Gallipot was subsumed into a new Regency house, retaining the old kitchen. Documentation of the house is rare. The most instructive depiction is from an incidental detail in a Victorian print of the square, which shows Suffolk House in the background (left). Besides the bows, the other dominant feature of the façade was the twenty-six windows, some of which are just visible in the extremely rare photograph of Suffolk House in 1920 (opposite, bottom). All that survives is a crumbling, once stone-clad, brick boundary pier on the Suffolk Square side (right). Studying the 1809 and 1820 map of Cheltenham, it is clear that Suffolk House remained a peninsula into virgin land before being successfully integrated into the present square, during the 1820s and 1830s.

Harley Lodge, Tivoli Circus. Harley Lodge, later The Crossways, stood on a peculiar wedge-shaped site bound in by Andover Road and Tivoli Circus. It was a stuccoed Regency house, built before 1834, consisting of three bays and two storeys, with a double French window wing to the left, and a wing to the right. Harley Lodge had a central porch with 'Soanean' incised corner columns, side lights and moulded entablature. The house also featured full height pilasters at either end of the façade, which supported a moulded entablature. It was approached by a garden path and had a front lawn, walled garden, summerhouse and a yard at the rear of the property. Architecturally it was similar to other houses in the Tivoli area of Cheltenham. Harley Lodge was demolished in the 1950s, thus enabling the A40 to be widened.

The Casino, Painswick Lawn. The Casino, despite its striking name, must be among Cheltenham's most obscure demolished buildings. It was built for a William Whitehead. The only known documentation is in S.Y. Griffith's *New Historical Description of Cheltenham* (1826). If it was not for this engraving, The Casino would have almost certainly been completely forgotten. Griffith's view depicts a very plain box-like two-storey villa, five bays wide and four bays deep, with a projecting porch to one side. It was 'just completed' in 1824 with '14 rooms: coach house and stables'. More tantalising, however, is an 1825 description of a 'roomy entrance hall, with marble dotted floor, and Bath stone geometrical staircase'. The Casino was blandly renamed Haldon House during the Victorian period. The house was demolished in the 1930s; nevertheless, a boundary wall pier survives on the corner of Painswick Lawn and St James' Place (shown opposite). Fortunately the Casino's racy name has been preserved in Casino Place – albeit a muddy track running along the former back of the property.

Griffith's view is also instructive in that it shows the surrounding countryside completely free of any neighbouring properties, prior to development, in the late 1820s and 1830s, into the present Tivoli district of Cheltenham. In the background, on the right, is an uninterrupted, distant view of Leckhampton Court and the parish church.

Woodlands, The Park. There is an intriguing lacuna of forty-one years between the proposal of Woodlands, in 1833, and its eventual erection in 1874. A hiatus like this might well be unique in Cheltenham's history. Woodlands and its grounds, possibly the largest private garden ever in Cheltenham, appears to have been first delineated on an 1833 plan of the Park Estate. However, nothing happened until P.H. Jackson built a house on the site in 1874. Jackson embellished an atmospheric Gothic Revival property with a lodge, wilderness, footbridges, a lake based on a pre-existing fish pond and a boat house. In 1885, just over a decade after it was built, Woodlands was on the market and advertised as having, among other features, a 'Conservatory, with Fountain fitted'. The house was 'approached by a long Carriage Drive from the Public Road, with Entrance Lodge'. Later still sale particulars for the lost house describe it as being a 'picturesque gabled creeper and ivy-covered Residence'. It is curious to reflect that had the house been built in 1833 it is likely to have been in the late neo-classical style – perhaps a Greek Revival essay; however, by 1874 taste had moved so far that it was executed in the High Victorian Gothic Revival manner. Woodlands, and its 23 acres, was purchased by Gloscat, in an earlier incarnation, in 1938. The house was demolished in about 1955.

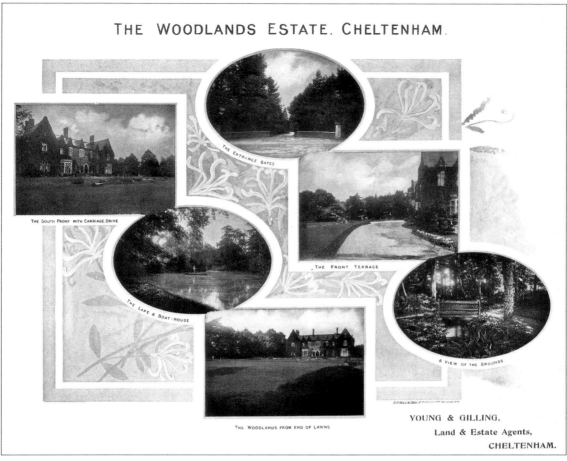

THE WOODLANDS ESTATE. CHELTENHAM.

THE ENTRANCE GATES

THE SOUTH FRONT WITH CARRIAGE DRIVE

THE FRONT TERRACE

THE LAKE & BOAT-HOUSE

A VIEW OF THE GROUNDS

THE WOODLANDS FROM END OF LAWNS

YOUNG & GILLING,
Land & Estate Agents,
CHELTENHAM.

Tudor Lodge, The Park. The Park Estate was purchased by Thomas Billings in 1831. In 1833–4 Billings laid out what was briefly to become the Gloucestershire Zoological, Botanical and Horticultural Gardens, which had failed by 1838. The land was then sold to the Gloucester architect Samuel Whitfield Daukes, who converted it into public pleasure grounds and developed villas around the perimeter. One of these villas was Tudor Lodge, which was designed and built by Daukes for G.W. Thomson in 1837. An 1884 sale particular described the house thus: 'The Residence was built under the superintendence of the well-known Architect, the late S.W. Daukes, Esq., as a specimen of the Tudor style of architecture, and the details are carried out in the strictest manner.' The grounds were quite large, with an ornamental rock garden and summerhouse.

In 1952 Bryan Little noted that 'one of them [the houses at The Park] by Daukes himself is a strange Gothic cuckoo in this Grecian nest that goes by the name of Tudor Lodge and has a few stylistic brethren in other parts of Cheltenham'. Matched only by Abbeyholme, Cheltenham's most elaborate Gothic Revival house was shamefully demolished in 1966 and replaced with the most dull Modernist blocks imaginable. The developers thoughtfully spared a single polygonal boundary pier, which is in the same style as the demolished house.

Lodge Gate. In 1842 the former Gloucestershire Zoological, Botanical and Horticultural Gardens were reopened as Park Gardens, under the ownership of the architect Samuel Whitfield Daukes. Park Gardens were put up for auction in 1844. In 1854 the gardens were sold once again and split into two properties, which were to become Fullwood Park and Broadlands. Lodge Gate, a 'purely Italian' design, was erected in 1839 'from the design of Mr. S.W. Daukes', and was described in 1844 as a 'handsome lodge, in the character of an Italian villa'. Lodge Gate's architecture was emphatically Italianate and is typical of the incorrigibly eclectic Daukes. The lodge stood just west of the present Fullwood Lodge and carriage sweep. Daukes's lodge disappeared sometime after 1870, suggesting that it had had a life of little more than thirty-one years.

Mystery building. What could be more quintessentially Cheltenham than this small mansion set within spacious grounds? And in what part of town was this villa – if Cheltenham at all? It is generally agreed that the building in question has the ambience of a house set in the Park area of town. Could it have been one of the seven demolished Park houses, which were Virginia Water, Woodlands, Woodleigh, St Clair, Tudor Lodge, Lyncourt and Belfont? The appearance of Virginia Water, Woodlands and Tudor Lodge is known, but documentation of the other four has always been elusive. This attractive lithograph was made by George Rowe, originator of 653 known prints, sixty-five of which were of Cheltenham. With its appliqué Doric classicism and bland proportions, is this late Regency box so far removed from the Bovis homes of today?

VIRGINIA WATER   IN THE **PARK**   CHELTENHAM

Virginia Water, Park Place. As previously mentioned, the laying out of the Park Estate by Thomas Billings began in about 1831. At its height, before the twentieth-century demolitions, the estate boasted thirty-seven villas in all. Virginia Water was a large property on the corner of Park Drive and Park Place. It was built between 1831 and 1833 on a 3¼ acre site by one Cornelius Blackwell, who was acting only as a trustee for Billings, and as such was the first house to be built at the Park. The above view is a vignette taken from an 1833 plan of the Park Estate; underneath is a caption reading 'Designed by T. Billings', which might well suggest that he was therefore the architect of Virginia Water. In 1833 Virginia Water's grounds were largely filled with a 'double lake', which featured an island, and a secondary lake which passed beneath Park Place and into the grounds of the current Mercian Court. The point where the lake passed under Park Place was marked by a bridge; only one side of the balustraded parapet survives, in front of Mercian Court. In 1901 the house, which had ten bedrooms, 13-foot-high reception rooms and a garden, by then of 2½ acres, was put on the market. The house, known successively as Virginia Water, Boteler House and Ferniherst, was demolished in about 1959 and replaced with Eric Lyons's Park House flats of about 1960.

Old Arle Court Lodge, close to the Tewkesbury Road. The above photograph was taken in February 1972. Thomas Butt purchased the Arle Court Estate in 1795 and died at Old Arle Court in 1828. According to a 1913 source there were 'two Georgian lodges (very seldom recognised), one on and one near the Tewkesbury Road, both built by the first Mr. Butt [Thomas] at the beginning of the last century'. The above lodge connected Old Arle Court – the remains of which still exist on Kingsmead Road – with the Tewkesbury Road by way of an elm-lined avenue, which crossed the River Chelt. References to Old Arle Court can be traced back to 1605. Conventionally Greek Revival from the angle in the above photograph, the lodge was in fact an ungainly sprawl, with its late nineteenth- or early twentieth-century extensions, which could be better seen from the Tewkesbury Road. This once-stylish lodge, with its portico and fluted Doric columns *in antis*, is somewhat reminiscent of the charming canal lodges, designed by Robert Mylne, on the Gloucester to Berkeley Canal.

Arle House, Village Road, Arle. Although not strictly in Cheltenham, Arle House represents the western extremity of this survey. When Arle House was built in 1826 it was, with its Elizabethan neighbour Arle Court, the focal point of a tiny hamlet still very much in the countryside and quite separate from nearby Cheltenham. The hamlet of Arle was absorbed into the suburbs of Cheltenham in the 1950s, and in the process lost its historic identity.

Arle House was built for John Gregory Welch and illustrated in S.Y. Griffith's *New Historical Description of Cheltenham* (1826), and was rumoured to have cost £16,000. In 1854 it was described thus: 'It presents a handsome square edifice, stuccoed in imitation of stone. The south front decorated by a projecting porch, standing upon a Flight of Steps, and surmounted by a Verandah, and forming the Principal Entrance to the house.' The focal point of an otherwise austere façade was the Tuscan porch (accessed from the sides) of four columns on a rusticated base, which is continued along the façade as a plinth. Above the porch's entablature is a canopy supported by decorative iron-work – as would have been found in Cheltenham itself at the time. The canopy sheltered a French window which led out on to the top of the porch. This must have once been a delightful summer seat with views over the hamlet, the countryside and perhaps Regency Cheltenham in the distance.

According to sale particulars there was 'a paved hall, with folding entrance doors', a drawing room with 'statuary marble chimney piece' and a 'veined black marble mantel piece' in the dining room. The house was the centre of a 326 acre estate and two farms. The Welch family continued to live at Arle House until 1945; it was demolished in about 1960, and in 1961 replaced by an architecturally nondescript old people's home.

Lansdown Terrace, Malvern Road. Let us draw to a close on a more positive note. Arguably Cheltenham's grandest terrace ever, Lansdown Terrace, designed and built by R.W. Jearrad, a London-based architect, was 'rapidly advancing' by 1832 and complete to no. 23, the above house, by 1840. This free-standing terrace house – surely a contradiction in terms – was the start of a proposed second range of twelve houses extending towards Christ Church. No. 23, started after 1834, even has the aborted elevational mouldings of its intended neighbour, towards the left of both pictures. Here is a graphic example, if one was ever needed, of Cheltenham's Regency booms and busts. David Verey considered Lansdown Terrace 'indubitably the most original terrace in Cheltenham'. By the early 1990s no. 23 was derelict but fortunately it was rescued from the brink at the end of the decade, and restored by Ladley Associates Architects in conjunction with English Heritage.

PICTURE CREDITS

Oliver Bradbury: pp. 13 (bottom), 15 (bottom), 16–17, 20 (bottom), 24 (bottom), 27 (bottom), 31 (bottom), 36, 40 (bottom), 41 (bottom), 44 (bottom right), 45 (bottom), 47 (bottom), 51 (bottom), 52 (inset), 53 (inset), 54 (bottom), 57, 70 (bottom), 72 (inset), 75 (bottom), 86 (bottom), 93, 100 (bottom), 107 (bottom), 110 (bottom), 111 (bottom right), 115 (bottom), 116 (inset), 117 (bottom), 121, 122 (bottom), 131 (bottom), 132 (bottom), 133 (bottom), 141, 143 (both bottom), 145, 147 (bottom), 149, 150 (bottom), 153, 155 (bottom), 157, 158–9, 161, 163 (bottom), 168 (bottom), 172, 174.

The author would like to thank the following for their permission to reproduce photographs: **Barnard & Partners**: pp. 138 (top), 139; **Kath Boothman**; p. 128; **Amina Chatwin**: pp. 50 (top), 104 (top), 169 (top); **Cheltenham Art Gallery and Museum**: pp. 14, 18 (top), 19 (top), 20 (middle), 21 (top), 22, 23 (top), 24 (top), 25 (top), 32, 33 (top), 39 (top), 40 (top), 41 (top), 42 (top), 45 (top), 46, 47 (top), 53, 58 (top), 62 (top), 66 (top), 69 (top), 71 (top), 75 (top), 76 (top, photograph by Steven Blake), 80 (top), 87 (top, Steven Blake), 89 (top), 90 (top), 94 (top), 95 (top), 100 (top), 102, 108, 109 (bottom), 112, 114, 117 (top), 120 (bottom), 122 (top), 123 (top), 130–1, 140, 143 (top), 150 (top), 155 (top), 156 (top), 160, 167; **Cheltenham College Archives**: pp. 154 (top), 147 (top); **Cheltenham Ladies' College**: p. 133 (top); **Cheltenham Library Local Studies Collection**: pp. 1, 13, 18 (bottom), 20 (top), 26 (top), 27 (top), 43, 48 (top), 52, 54 (middle), 55 (top), 56, 58 (bottom), 60 (top), 64–5, 68 (top), 70 (top), 72, 74, 77 (top), 78, 82 (top), 85 (top), 88 (top), 91, 94 (bottom), 97 (top), 105 (top), 118, 132 (top), 136 (top), 137, 142 (top), 144, 156 (bottom), 164, 166 (top); **Corpus Christi College, Oxford**: p. 2 (Oxford CCCA/Fe 42/1); **Gloucestershire County Record Office**: pp. 28 (D3867/IV/2711), 38 (top) (D1799 Z5/74), 44 (top) (D303 P5), 61 (top) (A78/57), 66 (bottom) (D3867/IV/848), 92 (D3867/IV/35/DN/12), 96 (D2593 2/702), 98 (D3867/IV/9997), 99 (top) (D3867/IV/9998), 106 (bottom) (D3867/IV/15176), 124 (top) (D1388/SL 6/89), 125 (top) (K851/2), 126 (D3867/IV/12099), 146 (top) (D3867/IV/10413), 162, 163 (top) (SL35), 168 (top) (D303/P5); **Joan Halling**: p. 81; **John Murray**: p. 111 (bottom left) (taken from John Betjeman, *First and Last Loves*, John Murray, 1952); **National Monuments Record**: pp. 30, 51 (top right), 86 (top), 107 (top), 148, 151 (top), 152 (bottom), 170; **National Railway Museum, York**: pp. 34–5; **Bonnie Nichol**: p. 116; **Nigel Temple**: pp. 17 (top right and bottom), 19 (bottom), 20 (bottom), 23 (bottom), 25 (bottom), 26 (bottom), 29, 31 (top), 33 (bottom), 38 (bottom), 39 (bottom), 42 (bottom), 43 (inset), 44 (bottom left), 48 (bottom), 50 (bottom), 55 (bottom), 59, 60 (bottom), 61 (bottom), 62 (bottom), 65 (top), 67, 68 (bottom), 69 (bottom), 71 (bottom), 76 (bottom), 77 (bottom), 79, 80 (bottom), 81 (bottom), 82 (bottom), 85 (bottom), 87 (bottom), 88 (bottom), 89 (bottom), 90 (bottom), 95 (bottom), 97 (bottom), 99 (bottom), 101, 103, 104 (bottom), 105 (bottom), 106 (top), 109 (top), 111 (top), 113, 115 (top), 119 (top), 120 (top), 123 (bottom), 124 (bottom), 127, 129, 134, 135, 136 (bottom), 138 (bottom), 142 (bottom), 146 (bottom), 151 (bottom), 152 (top), 154 (bottom), 165, 166 (bottom), 169 (bottom), 171; **V&A Picture Library**: p. 110 (top) (E. 1308: 74–2001).

Whitbread tower, Monson Avenue. And, finally, a triumph for those lovers of *Morality & Architecture*. The above eight-storey office block, built for Whitbread Plc in 1966 by Gotch & Partners of Bristol, was never a loved Cheltenham landmark and so few will be sorry to see its downfall. It was built on the site of Monson Villa (an early villa of *c.* 1805), the home of the Hon. Miss Monson, builder of nearby St Margaret's Villa (destroyed in December 1940) and St Margaret's Terrace. No view of Monson Villa has ever come to light and it was probably demolished in the late nineteenth century. The Whitbread tower, with its curtain windows and clichéd employment of 'fins' on a lower adjoining section, was an archetypal 1960s building. Arguably it could have been worse and have had a raw concrete facing. The real culprit, however, is the Eagle Star building of 1968 on Bath Road, though saying that, the Whitbread tower must have inaugurated the unfortunate and short-lived spree of Cheltenham tower building in the late 1960s. However, knowing the poverty of new architectural design in Cheltenham at the moment, the tower's replacement is unlikely to be an improvement on what was here already.

INDEX